The River Cottage

Outdoor Cooking Handbook

The River Cottage
Outdoor Cooking
Handbook

by Gill Meller

with an introduction by
Hugh Fearnley-Whittingstall

rivercottage.net

BLOOMSBURY PUBLISHING
LONDON · OXFORD · NEW YORK · NEW DELHI · SYDNEY

For my fire – Alice

BLOOMSBURY PUBLISHING
Bloomsbury Publishing Plc
50 Bedford Square, London, WC1B 3DP, UK

BLOOMSBURY, BLOOMSBURY PUBLISHING
and the Diana logo are trademarks of Bloomsbury Publishing Plc

First published in Great Britain 2019

A catalogue record for this book is available from the British Library

ISBN: HB: 978-1-4088-7348-9

2 4 6 8 10 9 7 5 3 1

Project Editor: Janet Illsley
Designer: Will Webb
Photographer: Gavin Kingcome
Indexer: Hilary Bird

Printed and bound in Italy by Graphicom

MIX
Paper from
responsible sources
FSC
www.fsc.org   FSC® C013123

To find out more about our authors and books visit www.bloomsbury.com and sign up for our newsletters

Contents

Open-fire cookery has always been integral to the River Cottage

way of doing things. It's been integral to my way of doing things for even longer. From foil-wrapped baked spuds or bonfire night chipolatas on sticks (pre-cooked by Mum for safety, I suspect), to my first driftwood-fired, self-caught mackerel, the crackle of a campfire has been, for me, a sign that food is about to gain an extra dimension of deliciousness.

I think it's indisputable that the touch of scorching, blistering heat and the kiss of smoke that you get from an open fire can do extraordinarily good things to food. It's true for fish, fowl, flesh and – increasingly for me these days – for vegetables and even fruit too. There is something elemental about open-fire cookery; it's so simple. The cooking method itself supplies the flavour and the seasoning – you really don't need to mess about too much with complicated condiments or multiple side dishes. And, of course, most food cooked out in the fresh air is eaten out in the fresh air too, which just adds to the pleasure. It's a way of cooking that fits perfectly with the ingredients I want to eat – fresh, seasonal, unpretentious.

This natural sympathy between menu and method is something that Gill Meller clearly understood instinctively when I first met him, almost 20 years ago. He joined me at the first River Cottage HQ, outside Bridport, as a very young but very talented chef and it wasn't long before we were experimenting gleefully – not just with what we cooked but how we cooked it. In this book, Gill describes the first two wood-fired ovens that we built and how we learned to get amazing food out of them. I have many other happy memories relating to our open-fire forays: fire-roasting an entire deer for a wedding, lining up 20 chickens on a single spit, cooking over countless beach barbecues and even getting a curious, rotating cage made for us by a local blacksmith. We used the cage for roasting vegetables over open flames, turning it on a handle like a tombola drum, and tumbling and toasting the veg inside. The results, in all cases, were absolutely delicious.

In open-fire cookery, as in many other things, Gill and I became partners in crime, egging each other on to try new things. We discovered it was possible to turn almost any non-flammable container, from a washing-machine drum to an old galvanised feed trough, into a very serviceable barbecue. Several such barbecues, we found, could be hauled on board a small fishing boat, which made us particularly happy. The joy of watching the sun go down on the water while you grill fish so fresh that it's barely stopped moving is hard to describe.

Gill and I also learned that there aren't many things you can't cook on an open fire if you turn your mind to it. Oysters and mussels? No problem. Lettuce and spring onions? Absolute doddle. Bread? Fantastic. Roots and brassicas? Why ever not? You can bring the alchemy of fresh air, smoke and glowing embers to bear on almost anything you fancy – you just need a modicum of imagination and enough space to fire up a pile of sticks.

This spirit of enterprise is one of the things I love about outdoor cooking – coupled with the sheer fun of it. You've got to relax in order to enjoy it. Cooking outdoors is often a little rough around the edges, but the lack of finesse is liberating. You can forget about exact timings, precise temperature control and perfect presentation. Though it must be said that watching the food is important. I once baked a shepherd's pie in a Dutch oven over a campfire for a bunch of allotment holders, confident that half an hour would do it. But after just 15 minutes, I discovered that my pie was already burnt on the top and bottom. Fortunately, it was the edible kind of burnt that can be forgiven with a good supply of cold beer.

Nine times out of ten, the reason for this kind of 'over-charring' is that the cook has simply wandered off. Open-fire cooking does not demand a great deal of skill or technique, but it does ask for your attention. However, in my book, that is just one more thing in its favour. It's a very mindful kind of process.

As a nation, I think we have developed a rather debilitating nervousness around the idea of outdoor food. Many cooks only ever cook indoors. Others who do light up the barbie stick very closely to their burgers-and-bangers comfort zone. If that's the case for you, you may be missing a trick. There is a whole world of flavour to be discovered when you start throwing new things onto the grill, or into a wood-fired oven. And there are all sorts of ways to circumvent any anxieties you might have. An accurate probe thermometer will help you ensure that your meat is cooked through. Nifty kit such as grilling baskets make it easy to turn food without sticking. And this book will arm you with all you need to know about fire-building, heat management and, of course, the best kind of open-fire recipes.

At the end of the day, come rain or shine, beach or back garden, I'm pretty sure Gill would always rather cook outdoors than in. And that means these recipes come from a place of real passion and enjoyment. It also means they are well tested and fully approved by the many fortunate friends, colleagues and family members who get to try them. The dishes you'll find here are original, sometimes surprising, but often beautifully simple. As with all Gill's food, they are rooted in time and place, seasonality and the moment, designed to bring the very best out of good ingredients, never to disguise or complicate them.

Gill's love of open-fire cookery has never abated. In fact, I think it grows by the year. As he explains, for him it's not just about the food, it's about the life-enhancing effects of being deeply involved with what you eat and the environment you eat it in. I'm quite sure that this commitment to real food and hands-on cooking, along with Gill's unceasing fascination with flame and smoke, will rub off on you when you delve into these pages. So read on, and I'm sure you will find your interest kindled and your enthusiasm fired!

Hugh Fearnley-Whittingstall, East Devon, January 2019

Fire Basics

Cooking over fire is, for me, one of the simplest and best ways to enjoy food. I've always been excited by fire. At the age of seven, I was cooking grass on my campfire – as you do – using the classic recipe whereby grass and rainwater are combined in an old pan and boiled for hours. At some point and for no reason I can recollect, I reached out and picked up a white-hot stone from the base of the fire. Of course, I burnt my hand, and I shot off round the garden like a missile. I remember my grandfather giving me £5 to stop crying; I was really grateful, but it hurt so much I couldn't.

This rather heated early experience did not make me fear fire. Quite the reverse: I've been cooking stuff over fire in one way or another ever since. Fire and smoke have weaved though my life in all sorts of wonderful ways. I'm pleased to say my repertoire of recipes has improved (they are nearly all edible now), and I'm finding new, exciting ways to develop open-fire cooking all the time.

As a chef I've had the good fortune to cook in lots of fantastic kitchens. But cooking outside over wood or charcoal is something completely different. It's far more engaging. It allows you to forge a connection with the food you eat that you could never make using only a fan-assisted oven inside a house or a restaurant.

It goes without saying that you have to spend some time learning how to cook over an open fire. It's not like switching on an induction hob and waiting for a timer to beep. Open-fire cooking is a craft, an ancient art. But the time and energy you put into this learning will give you rich rewards. For a few hours, you can escape the boundaries of convention and slip the tethers of time. There's a freedom in outdoor cooking that means recipes loosen and become simply ideas. The cook becomes, primarily, a manager of heat, judging and adjusting distance and temperature and time. Rain and sun are simply elements to balance against the energies of wood and charcoal.

Cooking outside over an open fire helps you unlock instincts and hidden skills you may never have thought you had. You learn basic science, you learn about temperature, weather and wind. You learn about trees and the seasons. You learn how one action affects another and how small decisions can often have big, flavoursome outcomes. Beyond this, I think you learn something about yourself and the environment you live in, as well as your place in it. And that, to my mind, is a very good thing.

River Cottage has been key to all this for me. Cooking alongside Hugh and the talented chefs at Park Farm has cemented my understanding of over-fire cookery. Whether blistering a pizza in the sixteenth-century farmhouse wood oven, roasting a whole pig for a celebratory feast or barbecuing mackerel for groups of keen students, my time here has taught me the beauty of these primal skills and given me the confidence to serve real, ethically produced food, straight from the fire, whenever I can.

All of this contrasts rather starkly with the way we typically eat these days. The industrialisation of food production and the development of processed ingredients and ready meals means that we in the Western world don't cook anything like as much as we used to – indoors or out. This modern way of eating has all sorts of environmental, social and health-related ramifications – but on top of that, it means that much of the everyday cooking we do has lost its fun. Half the time there's no thinking involved, no romance, no spirit, no effort, no grit, and often little reward.

That's not to say that open-fire cooking isn't still being practised. It is – every day, across the globe and in every which way you can think of. For some cultures, in some parts of the world, it is part of daily routine. We just don't do it enough here, and I hope this book will go some way towards changing that.

In these pages, I'll go over the fundamental principles of outdoor cooking, and give you an understanding of the variables involved. We'll look at some of my favourite approaches to outdoor cooking, as well as methods and techniques from around the world, from the earth ovens of the Māori in New Zealand to the smoky, sticky depths of American Deep South barbecues. I'll explain how to cook in wood ovens, as well as truss a pig for spit-roasting, bake fish and vegetables in clay, and cook directly in the embers themselves.

A lot of the techniques and recipes I'll share are easy – but don't be deceived into thinking they are insignificant because of that. They represent a way out of our everyday lives, opening a door into a past many of us think we have no time for. I'd like to encourage you, wherever you are, to cook outside a little more often – to capture your imagination, and rekindle that spark which we all have somewhere within us.

Cooking with fire

Combustion (i.e. burning) is one of the most important chemical processes in the history of our universe. Fire flows through the ecological systems of our world like molten rock flows under the earth's crust, and it underpins the very fabric of civilisation, both ancient and modern.

According to many experts, the earliest definitive evidence of the controlled use of fire comes from the Wonderwerk Cave site, in the Northern Cape province of South Africa. The samples of burnt bone and plant ash found here are said to be more than a million years old.

The mastery of fire was a hugely important catalyst for human evolution. Initially, it gave our ancestors the means to cook meat and plants to make them more digestible, and there is a scientific argument that this was a key trigger for the development of the big, calorie-hungry brains that set us apart from other mammals. Fire provided warmth and light, which meant human activity could be extended into the night hours and that humans could move north, colonising places like Scandinavia, which were so cold and dark in the winter that otherwise they would have been uninhabitable. Fires brought people together, and offered them safety.

We continue to harness the power of fire, and not just for preparing a meal over or heating the house. Its influence is found in everything from industry to religion, from travel to agriculture, and from celebration to war. We live by fire and we die by it too. So when exactly did the Western world forget how to cook with it?

The answer is: very recently. From the Industrial Revolution onwards, fire was utilised in a whole new way, since it was the combustion of fossil fuels such as coal that helped to produce electricity. Natural gas, meanwhile, was refined to produce a domestic alternative to wood fuel. The electric cooker and gas hob became practical, clean and easy twentieth-century alternatives to cooking on an open fire.

I'm not against progress; times change, society changes. But in our digital age, things have altered beyond all recognition. Concrete jungles have replaced our woods. Our tools are now screens and computers, rather than axes. Our food is from factories, and our fires, for the most part, are not used to cook it. We are completely disconnected from our past, and from the land we have always lived on; and by losing our link with fire, I think we are, in some ways, disempowered and de-skilled.

One way to turn this around is to keep our old crafts and traditions alive, since so many of them are interwoven with fire and flame. Blacksmiths, woodsmen, charcoal burners, artisan bakers, potters and glass blowers all help us to re-forge a connection to our ancestors and to the rural past. I have huge respect for these crafts people and I think it's vitally important that we support them in the same

way we do our small independent shops, food producers, farmers and fishermen. It means the next generation will be able to benefit from their knowledge and skill, and enjoy the things they make.

But you don't have to be an artisan to tap into the ancient skills that are entwined with fire. Any cook can light a fire and find themselves drawn a little closer to a more natural, resourceful, self-sufficient way of life.

Fire, heat and smoke

A fire starts when heat is introduced to a flammable material (such as wood) and oxygen from the air. This is traditionally called the 'fire triangle', as fire cannot exist without the combination of heat, fuel and oxygen in the right proportions. The fire will be extinguished if you eliminate any one of these elements: remove the fuel and the flames will die because there is nothing left to burn, smother the fire and you cut off its oxygen supply, or douse it in water and you remove heat from the fire faster than heat is produced. In essence, fire is a living thing, just like us. If you take away food, air or warmth from human beings, our lights will go out in exactly the same way.

Once the fire is established it will be self-sustaining, provided there is a continuous supply of fuel and oxygen. This leaves the cook free to consider the two most important factors when cooking over fire: heat and smoke. These essential elements need to be understood, and managed to some extent, in order to get the best out of them.

Heat

Of course, the best thing about the combustion process is that it gives off heat. 'Heat' is simply energy transferred from something hot to a cooler object. The rate and manner in which that happens is infinitely variable – and essentially that's what cooking is.

All you need to do is learn to control heat (energy) to your advantage. We're fairly used to managing heat; we do it all the time. We do it with clothes, boots, hats and scarves. Constantly adjusting and tweaking our outer layers means that we can live comfortably in a range of temperatures, whether indoors or out.

Something as simple as running a bath involves managing heat too. There is some skill involved in blending the perfect ratio of hot and cold bath water, taking into account the various factors: how hot is the hot water? How cold is the cold? How much hot water is in the tank? What's the bath made of? Will someone be getting in after me, or with me? And so on. You get my point: we do all this without really thinking about it.

Outdoor cooking can become almost this intuitive. Managing heat on an open fire is not a complex thing. At it's most basic, it just means that if your food catches fire, you should put it out. In the event of your food catching fire, you will instinctively move it away from the high heat to a cooler place. That's lesson one in heat management. If, on the other hand, the food is not cooking at all, you'll move it closer to the heat. There's lesson two. When it is cooked, you remove it from the heat completely. That's three. The rest is just detail which we will get on to a bit later on in the book.

Smoke

Smoke is the heart and soul of outdoor cooking. It will tell you everything you need to know about your fire. Every curl is a signal, every puff an indication of what's happening below the grill. Smoke will hold your hand and take your food on a journey into new realms of deliciousness.

Smoke is a by-product of combustion, a combination of airborne solid and liquid particles. To understand the flavours created by wood smoke, it's helpful to know a little about the structure of wood.

Wood is composed of three main organic compounds: cellulose, hemicellulose and lignin. All plants contain cellulose and most contain hemicellulose, but a plant only becomes 'woody' when it also contains lignin. (A compound, by the way, is a substance that can be broken down into different elements. In other words, its molecules comprise atoms from more than one type of element.) As wood burns, these compounds are released into the air in the form of carbon dioxide and other gases, water vapour and ash. On their journey from the fire to the food, they react, condense and alter in composition. In other words, they form new compounds.

The outdoor cook is interested in the flavour compounds that come from lignin. The main ones are syringol and guaiacol, compounds that are found in all wood and charcoal. Syringol gives grilled food its smoky aroma, and guaiacol gives it the smoky taste. There are other, more subtle compounds that can give further character and colour to barbecued meat, fish or vegetables. These include eugenol and vanillin (think cloves and vanilla).

Temperature has a real bearing on these flavours. If your fire is too hot, you will lose some lovely sweet flavour notes, but if it's too cool, you can end up with bitter, acrid, tarry flavours. The ideal combustion temperature, for maximum deliciousness, is 300–400°C – that is the temperature of the burning wood itself, not of the warm, smoky environment above it, which has a much lower temperature.

Different types of wood produce different kinds of smoke because they contain varying amounts of lignin. They'll also burn at different temperatures and have more or less moisture. As a result, each type of wood produces its own particular set of flavour compounds that will influence your cooking in its own way.

Wood

I'm really lucky to live amid trees. There are nine acres of deciduous woodland below my house, made up of beech, ash, oak and hazel, flanked by willow, maple and elder. When we moved here in 2014, the woodland surrounding the property had breached the loose boundaries that separated our garden from the wilds. Fourteen big, self-seeded ash trees cast a shady canopy over the old lawn, with its herb and flower garden, and although they were beautiful, they had to be felled.

Once felled, the trees' long trunks were left in a big old pile for a year. These were then cut to length with a saw, and split with an axe into logs. The logs were stacked out of the weather, to allow them to 'season'. Five years later I'm still burning that wood in our little wood burner and in my wood oven, and I feel profoundly indebted to those ash trees.

Since cutting the fourteen ashes, we've managed to plant as many new trees around the place, including three quince trees – quince is a fruit I'm particularly fond of. In time, we will plant more. I believe that if consumption and renewal are balanced then burning wood can be largely carbon neutral, because the carbon dioxide absorbed by young trees compensates for the amount that is released during burning. It's also worth mentioning that cutting down a tree and burning the wood releases a similar quantity of carbon dioxide into the atmosphere as the amount there would be if the tree had been left to die and rot.

Where to get wood

I love gathering my own wood for open-fire cooking. It's an incredibly rewarding thing to do and, of course, it can save the money you might otherwise spend buying logs and charcoal. Note, however, that it is illegal to gather any wood from land that isn't your own unless you have permission (see p.32). If you do have authorisation, then fallen twigs, branches and slightly heavier limbs are well worth picking up. In the warmer summer and autumn months these windfall branches are likely to be perfectly dry, and you could stack them under cover until you're ready to burn them.

It is more likely, though, that you'll be buying your wood from a supplier who specialises in turning felled trees into firewood (see Directory, p.248). There are small independent firewood suppliers all over the country who will deliver hardwood logs straight to your door by the load (the price should be based on cubic metres and not weight). This is a practical and cost-effective way of buying wood and I'd recommend it over purchasing the small netted or bagged logs you'll find, carrying a jaw-dropping price tag, at petrol stations or garden centres. It can pay to have an axe on hand if you're buying firewood from a supplier, as you'll be able to split the wood into the smaller pieces you'll inevitably need.

If you live rurally you might be able to buy 'green' (freshly felled) wood and cut and season it yourself at home. This is even more cost effective. Green wood is usually sold by the 'cord' – a stack measuring approximately 4 x 8 x 4 feet. It's up to you to saw it into rounds and split those rounds into smaller logs for firewood. The split wood needs to be stacked out of the weather in an airy place, and left there for as long as it takes to dry out ('season'), ready for burning.

Drying out wood

To get the most heat from your wood and to ensure it's burning as efficiently and cleanly as possible, as well as producing the right kind of smoke, it's essential that it is nice and dry. Wet wood burns at a far lower temperature then dry wood, gives off dirty smoke and is an absolute nuisance to light – and green wood can actually be made up of as much as 60% water.

The best firewood has moisture levels of less than 20% (the optimum is 15%). How can you test this? You can simply trust your firewood supplier and/or you can look for obvious signs. Cracks in the grain are a clear sign the wood has been well seasoned. Weight-to-size ratio can be a clue: if your logs feel unusually heavy for their size, then that weight may be made up of moisture. And, of course, the way they look, feel and smell will give you a good indication of how dry they are. Alternatively, you can invest in a moisture meter, a small digital device that will give you a read-out of the percentage moisture content. These are easy to use and relatively cheap to buy online, and will give you a fairly accurate reading.

Cutting kindling

In order to cut your own kindling, you'll need a sharp, heavy splitting axe as well as a smaller kindling axe or hatchet. You can pick these up from garden centres and DIY shops or from online suppliers (see Directory, p.248). Axes are great tools to have to hand; they're easy to look after and indispensable if you burn wood regularly, indoors or out.

I recommend using softer woods for kindling (pine or poplar, for example), as they are easier to split than the harder woods, such as oak or chestnut. Soft wood also ignites more quickly and burns hotter. Select medium-sized logs without knots and try to ensure they have a relatively straight grain and are no more than a foot or so in length. You'll also need to find a large, round and sturdy log, which will become your 'splitting log'. Stand this on its end, positioned on a firm, level piece of ground (if you were to split kindling directly on the ground, you'd drive your axe into the mud, which dulls the blade and dampens the force of the strike).

Stand the log you intend to split on its end, in the centre of your splitting log. Before you swing, make sure your hands and feet are a safe distance from the axe and ensure there's no one near you who could be hurt – either by the axe or by flying lengths of kindling. Bring the axe down on the log. If the axe sticks in the wood without splitting, lift the two up together and drive them down on the splitting log for a second time, or until the log concedes. Repeat this process several times, splitting the log into thinner and thinner pieces. As the pieces get narrower, they will become less stable, and eventually they won't want to stand up at all. At this point, switch over to the smaller kindling axe and continue the job with this. Do not hold the kindling steady with one hand while you bring the axe down with the other. One slip or misjudged swing could result in a nasty accident. It's better to hold the length of kindling in situ with another length of kindling (as shown), or tease the tip of the axe blade into the top of the kindling before bringing it down.

A medium-sized piece of firewood should give you a dozen or more pieces of split kindling. Each piece of kindling should be no thicker than 1–2cm and, for practical purposes, no longer than 30cm. If you get on a roll and want to carry on splitting, fill a basket, or make a big pile and store it out of the weather. Scraps of bark, twigs, leaves and dry sticks can all be added to the mix.

Different types of wood

Many deciduous trees (those that shed their leaves in the autumn) make excellent firewood. The magical oak is one of them. A very hard wood, its strength and durability as timber have made it one of the most important trees in the progress of Western culture. It is incredibly dense, so when it's dry it burns slowly and at a consistent, high temperature. The smoke has a delicate, honey-sweet quality and if you can track some down for cooking over, you should be very happy.

The majority of hardwoods are good for cooking: alder, ash, beech, birch, chestnut and maple will all burn beautifully, assuming they're dry. The wood from fruit trees is wonderful to cook over too. Apple, pear and cherry woods all produce a sweet and fruity, aromatic smoke. Some of the strongest smoky flavours come from non-native hardwoods, such as hickory and mesquite – popular choices for slow-barbecuing.

Many chefs and barbecue enthusiasts alike have their own favourite wood to cook over, as different woods will complement different foods. In my experience though, such differences are subtle and based on personal taste. It makes sense that the wood from fruit and nut trees lends itself to such things as gamey meats, good pork and earthy autumn vegetables – but the notion that these ingredients wouldn't be absolutely delicious cooked over another type of wood is nonsense.

There are a few types of wood that aren't suitable for cooking over, notably the softer evergreen woods such as pine, spruce and fir. These less dense woods can be very resinous, so they light easily and burn hot (therefore ideal as kindling), but they burn through quickly, leaving next to no embers. Also, their high resin content can produce tarry, sooty smoke and introduce acrid flavours to your food.

Charcoal

For many people who love to cook outside, charcoal is the 'go to' fuel. This is due, in large part, to its practicality: it's extremely user-friendly.

Charcoal is a solid, black, carbon-based material, made by heating wood or some other organic matter without exposing it to air. Making charcoal can take several days, during which time water and other volatile components, such as methane, hydrogen and tar, are burnt off. The resulting fuel, almost pure carbon, is very light – as little as 25% of its original weight. It burns cleanly and consistently and will give out almost double the heat that wood can.

Unfortunately, most of the charcoal we burn in Britain is imported, and the trees used to make the bulk of it are felled in tropical rainforests. This ultimately contributes to deforestation, which, of course, is a major environmental issue globally. The solution is to buy local. We've been making charcoal in Britain since the Bronze Age and the craft is still very much alive and well. Small independent charcoal burners are easy to track down and are producing quality lumpwood charcoal in an ethical and sustainable way. The wood comes from areas managed as coppices, with trees cut and re-grown cyclically, so that a continual supply of charcoal can be made.

Charcoal is easy to ignite. You will need a little tinder to get it going and then, once it's smouldering away evenly and producing nice clean smoke, or no smoke at all, it is ready to cook on. I'm not a fan of the poorer quality charcoal briquettes or similar 'easy-light' coals doused in chemical fuel. I believe it's much better for our environment, and for us, to keep things as natural as possible – particularly when it comes to cooking.

Charcoal is a pleasure to cook on because it burns so consistently. When it's hot, it is phenomenally hot, and for some types of open-fire cooking, that searing white heat is exactly what is required. At other times, when you need a less intense heat, a charcoal fire's ferocity can be tempered by limiting the oxygen it's burning. That is why, more often than not, I cook over charcoal when I'm using an enclosed barbecue (traditional or otherwise). By damping down the airflow or by partially or entirely covering the fire, you can reduce the temperature dramatically, achieving a gentle, yet consistent, heat output.

Gas

Bottled gas, or LPG (Liquefied Petroleum Gas), is a mixture of hydrocarbon gases, extracted from petroleum or natural gas, in a liquefied form.

Gas is, of course, a fossil fuel, which means it's a non-renewable resource. It is extremely popular as a domestic cooking fuel because it is clean, controllable, smokeless, flavourless, instant and efficient. It certainly has its place in the world of outdoor cooking, though perhaps it has less soul than wood or charcoal (I must admit that I favour the latter).

Using a gas barbecue or burner can be incredibly practical. It enables you to cook outside wherever and whenever you want. Heat can be summoned almost instantaneously, and with the turn of a dial it can be adjusted from high to low. This is very convenient for the urban backyard, the cautious camper, or the climber on a tea break.

Many of the recipes in this book will work really well on a gas-fired barbecue, especially if the recipe is based on the principle of 'grilling over embers'. The gas flames heat the grill in the same way that wood or charcoal does, and that searing heat will cook the food in the same sizzling way. It's simple enough to drop the temperature by tweaking the gas flow if a recipe calls for a gentle approach, and what's more, many gas barbecues have lids that you can close, so slow cooking is also a possibility.

At the end of the day, if gas is your only option then go for it! You might sacrifice a little flavour, but you will still be enjoying the profound pleasure that outdoor cooking brings.

How to start a brilliant fire

Making a fire is simple. You just need the right things to be in the right place before you make a start. As with a recipe, there's no point in just chucking it all together any old how and hoping for the best. A little forethought pays off when you cook and it's exactly the same with a good fire.

I'll freely admit that I've felt the frustration that fruitless fire building can bring. The sense of failure can provoke irrational behaviour, but try to keep your head. Throwing reams of newspaper at it won't help, nor will the addition of a cereal packet or glossy magazine. Your thoughts are bound to drift towards highly flammable fuels, but that's not the way forward either – they'll only send you backwards (possibly even 6 feet downwards). Something as flammable as petrol is incredibly dangerous and should never be used to light any kind of fire, particularly not one you plan to cook over.

Instead, take time to do some forward planning. The first thing to consider is what you want to achieve at the end. If you're planning to cook a cow, you're going to need a pretty big blaze. But if you're just sizzling some sausages, a smaller, more manageable fire will be all that's required.

Then you'll need to consider where you want this fire to be, because once it's roaring away, it is impossible to move. Choose a safe, practical location for your fire (see p.32), but also one that is sociable. A fire way down the other end of the garden, miles away from your team and table, is no fire at all. One of the joys of outdoor cooking, after all, is the way it brings people together. It's in our nature to congregate around a fire.

Building a fire

Once you have established what your fire is for and where it's going to be, you can build it and light it. You will need to ensure that enough oxygen is able to get to the fuel once the fire is lit; this is why a lot of fireplaces in the home are set on a 'fire grate' that allows oxygen to be pulled up onto the fuel as it burns. If you're lighting your fire in a barbecue or wood oven or some other enclosed space, you need to take airflow into account. A lot of barbecues have dampers and vents that can be opened to increase airflow or shut to restrict it. Always open them when you light your fire.

Tinder, kindling and dry wood or charcoal are all you need to build your fire. I prefer not to use firelighters because I find that starting fires in the most natural way possible makes for more rewarding results. You'll also need matches or a lighter, of course, or a flint striker.

For me, tinder usually comes in the form of newspaper. Some people like to roll single sheets of newspaper into thin tubes then tie them in a basic loose knot, but

I prefer to scrunch up the sheets into loose balls before arranging them over the fire bed. I use standard broadsheet or tabloid newspaper, avoiding anything glossy, like magazines or brochures. You don't need excessive amounts of paper. As long as your kindling is nice and dry, and cut thinly, three or four full sheets of newspaper should be plenty.

You can use other materials as tinder, as long as they will take a flame easily, and burn hot and fast. Birch bark (from silver birch trees) makes wonderful tinder, for example. Thanks to its unusual papery layers, it can stay dry on the inside even if it's damp on the outside. It will ignite with the merest touch of a match, and may even take a spark from a flint striker. I've also used hay, dry gorse sprigs and straw to light fires before, as well as curled, dry tufts of coastal grass roots from the beach. The super-fine twirls of wood shavings sometimes used as packaging (called wood wool) make excellent tinder too.

Once you've arranged your tinder, be it scrunched newspaper balls or something else, it's time to top it with kindling – small pieces of wood. You can buy kindling – split, bagged and ready to go – or collect it yourself (from a place where you have permission to do so). Fallen twigs and thin branches work well as long as they are bone dry. Alternatively, you can cut your own kindling from dry logs (see p.21).

Arrange your kindling over the tinder in such a way that air can get in to the fire as you light it. I opt for a random scattering approach – two or three handfuls of kindling allowed to fall lightly on top of the tinder will do the job. Other, more structured methods include making wigwams of kindling or 'Jenga'-style constructions. Both work well.

One sure way to help things along is to use a sharp penknife to cut thickish wood shavings from smaller pieces of kindling. This creates a sort of intermediate fuel that forms a flammable bridge between the dry tinder and the larger kindling above. Simply run the blade down the wood in shallow strokes and you'll soon amass a handful or so.

Don't put any larger pieces of fuel on the fire before you light it, but make sure you have them – split logs or charcoal, dry branches and sticks – on standby. It's handy to have everything within reaching distance before you strike your light. Think of yourself as an architect; only when your foundations are solid should you consider building upwards.

The life cycle of a fire

Every fire starts off as a tiny spark, which, with time and sustenance, will grow. It can be maintained with feeding and attention until, when you have got what you need from it, you can let it die.

Lighting the fire The birth of a fire is the moment the dry tinder takes a spark. Use matches, a lighter or a flint striker to light your tinder in several places (pic 1). Make sure all these points are upwind of the greater mass of fuel, so that any breeze will fan the flames and direct them towards, rather than away from, the kindling. Young, popping flames will form and should spread quickly to the dry kindling, but there won't be much heat in the fire at this stage.

Letting the flames take hold If you have built your fire well, then within a few minutes everything will be alight. It's tempting to start piling on more fuel straight away but it's important not to rush. You need significant heat to build up within this young fire in order for it to grow, so look for signs that the kindling is burning really well before you add more wood. Does it look hot? Does it feel hot? Too much fuel, added too soon, will smother the fire.

Add fuel gradually and systematically, starting with relatively small pieces of wood or charcoal and placing them with care; fill the gaps, but let the flames breathe (pic 2). If you need a large, hot fire, take the time now to build it up gradually with plenty of fuel. Initially, the fire will produce unpredictable yellow flames and a thick white smoke as moisture and gasses are driven out of the fuel. The high heat you need for cooking is still a way off.

Hot embers and flames After a fairly short time, the kindling you started with will have burnt down to create a bed of hot embers. The larger logs placed on top should now be burning well and producing a high heat (pic 3). It's possible to begin cooking over the fire at this point – but not within the body of the flames, which will scorch and blacken the food. Utilise the heat by suspending food high above the flames, as with a spit-roast, or wait a bit longer until the flames have died down.

In some of the recipes for open-fire cooking, I have suggested that you gauge the temperature by hovering your hand above the grill and seeing how long it is before the heat forces you to move your hand away. If it's only about 1–2 seconds, that indicates a very high heat, good for searing.

Glowing embers When your larger logs have reached a point of full combustion, the flames will die back, leaving you with glowing embers: large lumps and smaller shards of carbonised wood (pic 4). The heat from this mass of hot embers is intense as well as consistent – the optimum conditions for most open-fire cooking. Now is

usually the time to get your grill over the embers and put some food on it. You can manage the heat by raising or lowering the grill, as well as raking embers around the bed of the fire. As the larger embers break up, their surface area increases and the heat they give off will initially rise; then the temperature will plateau. At this point, you'll probably be able to hover your hand above the grill for 2–4 seconds.

In order to maintain these optimum cooking conditions for any length of time, you'll need to feed the fire with more fuel. But you don't want to cause a big flare-up of flames. Add more dry wood to one side of the fire, and continue to cook over the existing hot embers while the new wood flames up. Once the new wood has reached full combustion and the flames begin to die back, you can rake the fresh, hot embers over the existing embers and keep cooking.

Embers to ash Eventually the embers will form a coating of ash with a fragile, dusty white appearance. The heat will still be intense but it will start to fall if no more fuel is added. Agitating or riddling the coals with a stick or poker will reinvigorate them and the heat will climb briefly before dropping off again. It's possible to utilise this gradually dissipating heat for slow cooking, or warming or drying food.

Cinders and ashes Once the fire is out, you will be left with burnt-out embers (cinders) and ash. If you plan to have more fires in the same place, it's worth leaving the cinders in situ: they'll make a good bed for your next blaze.

Extinguishing a fire properly

When the cooking is done, it is lovely to sit around a fire late into the evening and it's tempting to feed it to keep it going, but you should only do this if you know you'll be there for a while. If not, let it die down. Never leave a fire that's still smouldering. The rule is that if a fire is too hot to touch, then it's too hot to walk away from. This applies even in your own back garden, but especially if you've sited it in a wild place.

If you're not on your own property, you should extinguish any fire in such a way that it leaves no trace. It's always best to let a fire burn down naturally as much as possible before you finally extinguish it. You don't want half-burnt chunks of wood or charcoal lying about, especially in public places, and these can sometimes be smouldering within, even when they seem to be 'out'.

When your fire is down to embers, extinguish it by dousing it with plenty of water. Stir the water into the embers, which will help to expose any hotspots or embers that are still glowing. Keep dousing and stirring until the embers are cool. You can stir a little earth into the embers too, which will also help extinguish the fire (though don't bury the fire under a layer of earth, as this can actually trap the heat in and keep it burning).

When your fire is reduced to cool, wet ashes, and you have checked carefully for any stray embers that might have escaped from the main fire area, it's safe to leave. But if the fire was in a wild place, you should first scatter the ashes, away from the fire site, then cover over the fire site with earth so that no trace of it remains.

Careful practice, the law and safety

We should always be cautious of fire. It's an incredibly powerful force and often unpredictable, so it must be treated with respect. If you plan to cook outdoors it is worth getting to grips with some of the basics before you light the touch paper.

Lighting fires in public places
The best place to light an outdoor fire for cooking is your own backyard – whether that means your garden, or another piece of land that you own. This is because, with the exception of Scotland, you do not have the right to light a fire on any land in the UK without the owner's permission – and all land is owned by someone. This includes beaches, woodland, open access land and 'common land'. So even where you have the right to roam, you are still on someone else's turf.

That's not to say you can't get permission to light a fire on land you do not own, but you'll need to approach the landowner first. This could be the local council, the government, the National Trust, or a private individual. The local council is the best place to start, if you're unsure.

Remember that plenty of campsites allow fires and barbecues and will even sell you the wood you need to fuel them.

In Scotland, different laws mean you do have the right to light a campfire in many areas of open land, assuming you follow various sensible guidelines. Some areas are excluded, including forests and woodland, areas of special scientific interest, cultivated farmland and the like. You'll find full details of Scotland's Outdoor Access Code online.

Gathering wood
It's illegal to take fallen wood from any woodland in the UK without the permission of the person or body who owns the land. This is not a mean rule. Dead, rotting wood is an essential part of any woodland ecosystem, offering a habitat to many plants and creatures, and ultimately helping to generate new growth.

There are options, however. It is possible to buy a scavenging licence or permit for collecting wood on Forestry Commission land (apply to your nearest FC office). And on privately owned land, you may well be able to get permission from the landowner to collect a certain amount at certain times.

Managing fires safely

No matter where you light your fire, there are some very important common sense rules to be followed:

- **Keep fires small**, under control and constantly supervised.

- **Make sure the fire poses no danger** to people, property or animals.

- **Have a bucket of water** or a fire blanket to hand, with which you can quickly extinguish a fire if it looks like getting out of control.

- **Do not light fires** during a prolonged dry spell or anywhere near dry vegetation, such as dry grassland.

- **Never light fires** on peaty moor or heath land – these can get out of control and smoulder for days or even weeks, causing extensive damage.

- **Do not light fires** in woodland or on farmland.

- **If you've sought permission** to light a fire, then try to leave no traces afterwards (see p.30).

A bit of basic first aid

As with all cooking, it's possible to sustain the odd minor injury when working with an open fire. Burns are the most common incident.

Should you burn yourself, remove any clothing or jewellery from the affected area, head for the nearest tap and hold the burn under cool running water for at least 10 minutes (the NHS recommends 20 minutes). This effectively cools the burn site and minimises damage to the skin. Don't apply ice, lotions, creams, gels or anything greasy such as butter, all of which may increase the risk of infection.

Small, mild burns are best left to heal uncovered. Ordinary painkillers can help to ease any discomfort. But anything more serious should be covered with a sterile dressing while you seek medical help. Cling film is a good emergency dressing – discard the first few centimetres on the roll and take a clean piece from further in, then use this to loosely cover the burn. This will help prevent infection without sticking to the skin.

You need to seek medical help as soon as possible if the burnt area is bigger than your hand, or deep, or if you are showing signs of going into shock, such as clammy skin, sweating, shallow breathing, weakness or dizziness. Burns that show signs of developing an infection after a day or two also require medical treatment.

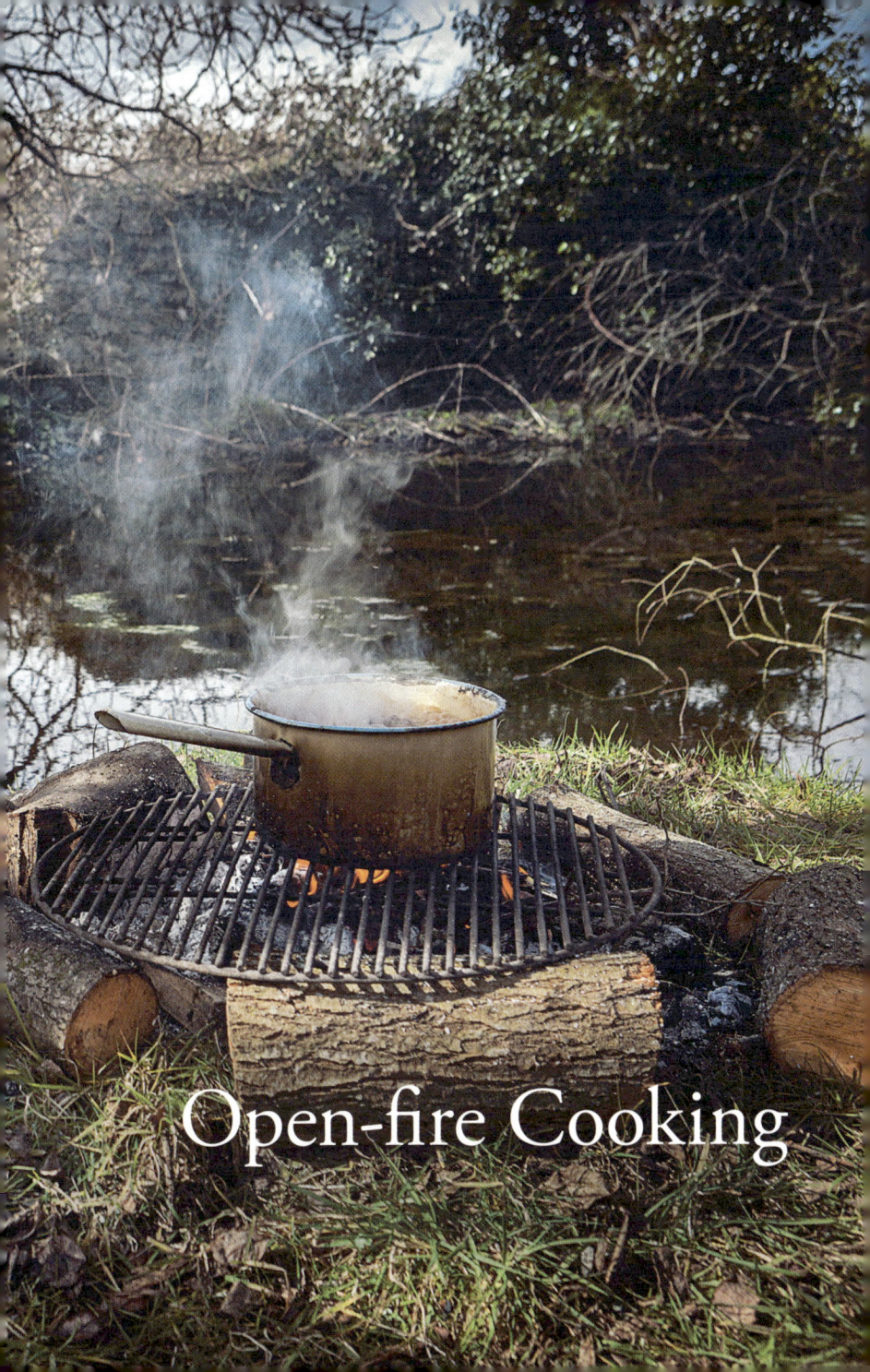

Open-fire Cooking

My favourite way to cook outside will always be the simplest way: over a wood fire on the ground. The attraction is in the little things – singed grass, steam from the earth, the crackle and whistle of twigs, the pop of stone and the smoke winding around me.

It's possible to cook literally anything on a wood fire on the ground. Having said that, trying to be too clever feels a bit 'antipyro' (my new word). There's a certain purity in the ancient art of cooking outdoors that I, for one, would never want to spoil. Save the complex, newfangled culinary stuff for a rainy day, when you're in your indoor kitchen, with your indoor stuff, thinking with an indoor mind. If an outdoor recipe calls for a blender, I would simply forget it.

I am tempted to suggest that, at least once, you flame-cook a meal for yourself and your friends using nothing but a stick. We should never underestimate the value of this ancient tool – to prod, to turn, to pierce, to spear and to eat from, it is one of the greatest and most indispensable of all open-fire utensils.

Food that has no need of knives or plates or forks can be the best kind. Imagine a Brussels sprout, for instance, on the end of that stick. It's first been turned in good olive oil then dipped into a coarse mixture of salt, pepper, crushed cumin seeds, chilli flakes and lemon zest before being roasted over the glowing embers of the campfire. Doesn't that make you want to eat sprouts right now? Or perhaps you'd prefer to start with a chunk of smoky, fatty, garlicky chorizo on your stick, before you spike the sprout. What joy as the sweet, salty fat renders and the sprout leaves char in the heat.

Simple stick cooking like this can easily be taken to the next level. Try it with a whole fish: push a stick into the fish's mouth and poke the other end into the ground at a 45° angle, then make a fire underneath; or twirl dough around a stick and hold it over the fire to cook. Or simply stick a stick in a good sausage and roast it gently over the fire until the skin begins to split and it's beautifully caramelised. This is the kind of washing-up-less heaven adored by children and adults alike.

I have a friend whose family walks during childhood would often begin with a campfire, into which all the children set jacket potatoes carefully wrapped in foil. The walk – a hearty one – would culminate back at the fire, where the children, as eager as they were hungry, lifted their potatoes from the cooling embers. Butter and salt and a good hunk of cheese made for a feast; I'm pretty sure regular baked potatoes from the oven wouldn't still be remembered with such fondness.

Experimenting with recipes

The recipes in this chapter cover a variety of techniques and approaches. And I want to reiterate that I'm using the term 'recipes' loosely. The notion of a 'recipe' is prescriptive by definition; it suggests that to stray or waver from the path is a sure road to ruin. Well, that is not the case in this book.

Please think of the following recipes as guides, designed to thrill and inspire, but open to interpretation, alteration, adaptation and revision. You'll notice that in most cases I do not give you exact cooking times or temperatures. Fire is just too consistently inconsistent. And I won't be choosing your fuel, or building your fire, smelling what you smell or tasting what you taste. If you're used to the safety of a conventional cookery book, you may find all this rather new. But I want you to have the confidence to rely on your senses to know that all is well. You'll learn through trial and error, through experiment and accidental discovery. The things you don't love, you won't do again, the things you do, you will – over and over.

The fire ring

Unlike a fire contained in a barbecue or wood-burning oven, fires on the ground can potentially spread. Placing a circle of large stones around a fire is a practical way to contain it. This 'fire ring' radiates and channels heat upwards, rather than outwards. It's ideal for propping up tools, resting grills or pans on, and bracing simple rotisseries, as well as for drying and even cooking on directly. Having a fire ring keeps your campsite or garden free from ash, embers, hot cinders, sharp bones and sticks, or the remnants of cooked food – and encourages a good fire bed too.

Beyond these practical benefits, fire rings have a deep-rooted ceremonial significance. The circle is an appropriate way to delineate a fire – the shape itself represents protection, totality, wholeness, timelessness, spirit, sun, self, the infinite, eternity and the continuous cycle of life. To define a space is to celebrate it, and over time many cultures and groups have done this with fire circles. The importance of the fire ring is recognised in ancient folk dances, modern pagan ceremonies, shamanic offerings and celestial tribal rituals. Regardless of the context, these fire circle celebrations always seem to help participants reach higher states and inspire them to live more meaningful, rewarding, creative and empowered lives. Cooking around the fire allows us to delve into this deliciously magical world and can inspire us in the same way.

When encircling your fire, bear in mind that some types of stone can split and crack when they get hot. Depending on where they are from and how they were formed, they may contain pockets of moisture or gas which, when heated, expand.

The results can be unsettling: the stones can split and break with some force, sending hot shards of stone whizzing about the place on occasion. Metamorphic rocks, such as quartzite, slate, granulite and schist, have been exposed to varying degrees of heat and pressure during their formation and should be safe to use. The same goes for igneous rocks, formed through the cooling and solidification of magma or lava – these include basalt, diorite and gabbro. Rocks more likely to explode include sandstone, limestone and flint.

If I can't find the right stones, I like to encircle a fire with logs or thick branches, which will restrict the fire until such time as they catch light. By then, the hot charred logs from the fire ring will be in a perfect state of flammability and can be chucked straight on the fire then replaced with new logs around the outside. Using green wood works a treat – it won't catch as quickly as seasoned wood, and gets a chance to dry out next to the fire.

Other ways to contain a fire

Stones and logs aside, it is, of course, possible to contain your fire in all manner of other ways. A conventional, garden-centre-style barbecue is one option – and any of the recipes in this chapter can be cooked on one – but at River Cottage, we love up-cycling, and we've tried and tested a weird and wacky selection of fire containers with mostly successful results.

Old tin buckets make great little portable fire containers, as do small farmyard animal troughs, washing machine drums, old chimney pots and car wheels (tyres removed). All these objects are a lot of fun to cook over, and it's great to give them a brilliant new purpose rather than sending them to the scrap heap.

Setting a grill over a campfire

The simplest option is to balance the grill on some logs. Three or four strategically placed hardwood logs offer the perfect platform on which to rest your grill. Yes, they will eventually catch fire but as long as the hot embers aren't touching them they shouldn't catch light quickly. If they do, simply replace them. Large stones make great props for grills, as do upturned terracotta flowerpots (as shown). A little tinkering with both the position of your chosen props and the grill may be required, but I find this approach less restrictive and more practical than most fixed grills you find on conventional barbecues. I like to ensure the grill is nice and hot before I set the food down on it. The searing hot bars channel heat right into the food and will leave char marks if the fire's hot enough. When the bars are hot, food is much less likely to stick to them too. Remember, the closer the grill is to the fire the hotter the temperature will be and the quicker your food will cook (and/or burn).

Barbecuing meat on an open fire

For many people, cooking outside is more or less synonymous with cooking meat. And although I'd urge anyone who enjoys open-fire cooking to branch out and discover the joys of smoky grilled fish, vegetables, bread and fruit as well, it's hard to beat some really good homemade burgers, smoky game or sweet, sticky ribs. There's just no oven, hob or grill that can equal the delicious flavours you can achieve with the heat and smoke from a wood or charcoal fire.

I believe that if we choose to cook meat for ourselves, our family and friends, then it should be produced in the most ethical, respectful and sustainable way possible. The meat from animals farmed on an industrial scale (the majority of meat we consume) is produced in unnatural, often cruel circumstances, but we, the consumers, have the power to change this through the choices we make. If we buy organic, free-range or wild meat, we send a clear message that factory farming is not acceptable to us.

Understanding meat

To understand how to get the best out of our meat when we cook it, we need to start by looking at the structure of animal flesh.

Let's begin with muscle tissue. In any animal, this is a collection of bundles of contracting fibres, made up of 'fibrils' (assemblies of proteins that work together to cause muscle movement). The density of these proteins makes meat highly nutritious. When heated, the proteins also develop the complex flavours that we love in cooked meat. However, muscle is also up to 75% water and cooking dries out and toughens the protein fibres. Some types of muscle dry out much more quickly than others.

In amongst the muscle fibres is connective tissue. This binds individual cells together, envelops larger groups of fibres, joins muscle sets together and also secures whole muscle sets to bones. The harder the muscle has to work in an animal, the more connective tissue is required to hold everything in place.

Collagen is the main structural protein found in this connective tissue, as well as in the skin, tendons and bones of animals. It is initially fibrous and tough, but when gently heated to a low cooking temperature, it partially dissolves into gelatine, which gets dispersed throughout the muscle. This gives the cooked meat a moist, tender texture.

Fat is another component of all meat. It can be found under the skin of an animal, as well as around the organs, between muscles and even dispersed throughout the muscle itself (known in butchery as 'marbling'). When cooked,

animal fat melts and lubricates the muscle, making the meat succulent. It also carries a great amount of flavour: the flavour compounds stored in the fat vary from species to species and are also heavily influenced by the animal's diet and the environment in which it lived.

We feed up our farm animals before we slaughter them, in order to build up fat. Wild animals carry different amounts of fat throughout the year. They are at their most vulnerable when their fat reserves are at their lowest (after a long winter, for instance) but we have learned to hunt them when their fat reserves are at their highest, after a summer of feeding.

When an animal is young, their muscle fibres are small in diameter, as they contain fewer protein fibrils. This less developed muscle is more tender to eat than the muscle from an older animal, which will have spent more time exercising and developed more protein fibrils within the muscle fibres. This is why young lambs are so tender in comparison to mutton, and why an old buck rabbit will take longer to stew than a sprightly young one.

In addition, within each animal there are some muscles that work considerably harder than others. A grazing animal, for instance, has strong, dense, hardworking neck and shoulder muscles, from the constant raising and lowering of its head. These muscles will have lots of bundled fibres, which in turn have plenty of collagen and fat reserves. Cuts of meat from these areas take longer to tenderise with heat, because they contain lots of connective tissue, but once that connective tissue dissolves and breaks down, they will eventually yield juicier, more succulent meat.

The hindquarter muscles from the same animals do less work in comparison, so they require less cooking. The least hardworking muscles, like the aptly named 'tenderloin' from a pig or the 'fillet of beef' from a cow – in both cases from the lower end of the back – have very little connective tissue and contain almost no fat. These cuts can be incredibly tender but may also become dry if they're cooked for too long, and they can lack real depth of flavour.

We don't always cut up a carcass into individual joints before cooking it, of course. Cooking a whole, large carcass, with its range of textures and densities, presents a special set of challenges, which are covered on pp.214–24.

A simpler proposition is to cook whole birds, such as chicken, pheasant or quail, over the open fire. You still need to factor in differing cooking times for the more tender and delicate breast meat and the denser, darker leg and thigh meat, but 'spatchcocking' the bird makes life much easier, allowing you to cook it from the underside for a longer time than on the breast side. Alternatively, you can remove the legs and cook them independently of the breast or 'crown'.

Marinades can help tenderise and moisten meat to some extent, particularly if they are based on something acidic such as wine, vinegar or yoghurt, which will slightly weaken muscle fibres. But I don't rely on marinades for this – they won't miraculously make tough meat meltingly tender. Good, well-produced meat that has been hung for an appropriate amount of time doesn't need tenderising – unless it's a naturally tough cut, in which case it requires slow cooking to do the job. I do like marinades from a flavour perspective, though.

Regardless of the cut, the longer you cook a piece of meat, the firmer it will become. When its core temperature reaches the 60°C mark, the majority of its proteins coagulate, or solidify, and the moisture that surrounds the muscle fibres starts to get squeezed out. The meat can still be juicy at this stage, but is starting to become dry.

When meat nears 70°C, the connective tissue that surrounds the muscle fibres shrinks rapidly, forcing the muscle fibres together and driving out the remaining moisture. The density of the muscle fibres at this stage makes it more difficult to cut across them, which makes the meat feel tough when you chew it, while the lack of moisture inside makes the meat taste dry in the mouth.

A tender cut of meat might be heading for ruination at this point, but for a tougher cut, it's a different story. Prolonged cooking in the temperature range 70–85°C causes collagen to dissolve into gelatine, softening and moistening the meat until it becomes 'fall-apart' tender. It is a lengthy process and the more connective tissue there is in the meat, the longer and slower the cooking needs to be. Pig's cheeks, for instance, are strong, powerful muscles, layered with fat and connective tissue. They can take hours of low, slow cooking to reach a stage where the meat falls temptingly apart. Ox tongue and lamb shanks are further good examples: muscles that never stop working, they start out incredibly tough but, when cooked until tender, they're unbelievably moist.

In minced meat products, such as sausages and burgers, the meat's structure has been completely changed. Mincing breaks up the muscle fibres so they don't contract in the same way when you heat them, and the fat is disbursed evenly, which means a burger or sausage remains moist throughout when it's cooked. Processed meat also tends to contain salt, which has a tenderising effect. These characteristics mean that your sausages and burgers will always cook evenly and consistently on a barbecue.

Flavour and barbecued meat

Exposing the surface of a piece of meat to searing heat results in something called the Maillard reaction: the sugars and amino acids contained in the meat combine to produce complex, meaty aromas, dark colours and savoury flavours. Couple this with the sweet aromas and flavour notes of wood smoke, and you begin to understand why cooking meat on an open fire gives us such delicious results.

Heat adds flavour in several other ways too. It will drive off water from the cooking meat, so its flavour will be intensified. In a rare or lightly cooked piece of meat, 'released' juices carry flavour onto your tongue as you chew. And in a slow-cooked piece of meat, meanwhile, heat causes changes to happen at a molecular level, producing more complex, deeper flavour notes.

We don't have to concern ourselves with seasoning ready-made burgers and bangers because as a general rule they have already been seasoned. But whole pieces of meat can be enhanced with salt, spices and other seasonings, or by a marinade laced with punchy aromatic ingredients that are used to baste the meat both before and during cooking. Basting meat as it cooks also slows the rate at which the meat's surface moisture evaporates: you're essentially creating a film or layer around the meat that helps to lock in moisture and develop flavour. I favour marinades containing at least some oil or fat, and sometimes I simply baste the meat with its own fat and juices.

How to avoid burning

Burnt meat (when the Maillard reaction goes too far) is one of the bigger obstacles we face when cooking over fire. Sometimes complete pyrolysis (carbonisation) occurs. This irreversible predicament is discouraging, but the good news is that it's wholly avoidable.

A vigilant eye and readiness to alter and regulate the heat source is key. Usually, it takes no more than minor adjustments to control the amount of heat reaching the meat and enable it to cook effectively, efficiently and accurately. You can raise or lower the grill, for example, or move the meat to a cooler spot on it. The burning fuel itself can be shifted or stirred to dissipate the heat a little.

If the fire is very hot and your options are restricted by a lack of any cooler spots on the grill, you can use tongs or a knife to remove the meat from the fire completely for a moment or two, before replacing it. Doing this for short intervals – and repeatedly, if necessary – stops the surface of the meat from over-colouring or burning before the inside is cooked to your liking.

Too much charcoal can produce a very high heat that is simply impractical to cook over. In this situation, remove the grill and, wearing a stout glove, use a metal shovel to transfer some of the burning charcoal into a metal bucket.

On an open grill, there is no way of catching the juices and liquid fat released during cooking. Fat is, of course, flammable so cooking fatty meats can cause the fire to flare up, as the fat renders and drips onto the coals. This just means that a little extra care is required. I find using a lightweight grill, such as an old wire cooling rack, to be a very good idea when cooking meat. This is really easy to lift off the fire should you get a flare-up.

Alternatively, spraying any flames with a mist of water from a plant-spray bottle will quickly extinguish them and, as long as your fire is substantial, it won't affect the cooking heat dramatically.

Checking if meat is done

The amount of fat, bone and skin, and the weight and shape of a piece of meat all affect how long it will take to cook – as does your cooking method. With such a panoply of variables, it can be hard to predict, timewise, when meat cooked over a fire will be done. Your senses – sight and touch – are usually a better way to ascertain 'doneness' than watching the clock. Does it look cooked on the outside? Has it developed a good deep colour? Is it hissing or spitting juice? Is the surface cracking, splitting or shrinking? When you touch the surface of the meat, does it feel firm? These external signs will give you a good indication of doneness, but only internal signs can confirm it.

You can get a good idea of how hot something is in the middle by inserting a small metal skewer or a thin paring knife, leaving it there for a few moments and then taking it out and touching it immediately (but cautiously!) to your wrist. If the metal feels uncomfortably hot, you can be pretty confident that the meat is done.

Using a digital probe thermometer is a more precise way to confirm that larger pieces of meat have reached the necessary core temperature – which will vary depending on the type of meat and the cut, as well as your own personal preference. Insert the probe into the deepest part of the meat (where heat will take longest to penetrate), and then refer to the guide on the opposite page.

Guide to cooked meat core temperatures

Make sure you insert the digital probe thermometer into the thickest part of the food to check the temperature. And remember, once the meat has come off the fire the residual heat or 'carry over cooking' can increase the internal temperature by 5–10°C within 5–10 minutes.

• **Beef and Venison**
  Rare 50°C
  Medium-rare 55°C
  Medium 60°C
  Medium-well done 65°C

• **Lamb and Goat**
  Medium 60°C
  Well done 72°C

• **Pork and Ham**
  Medium 60°C
  Well done 72°C

• **Chicken**
  Cooked through 72°C

• **Duck**
  Medium-rare 55°C
  Medium 60°C

If in doubt, the surest way to tell if your meat is cooked is to take it off the heat, cut into it and have a look. You'll be able to see if it's raw or underdone. Cutting into hot meat does, of course, cause some of the juices to flow out, but don't worry about this – the moisture loss will be insignificant compared to your peace of mind. And, of course, you can save the juices.

Resting meat

Most food benefits from a rest after it has been cooked, and with meat, resting is essential. It gives it a chance to firm up, which helps to trap some of the tasty, meaty juices in the fibres, making it more succulent. Resting also allows the meat to cool to a palatable temperature – one that allows you to really taste the meat. No food tastes its best when searing hot.

To rest cooked meat, transfer it to a warmed dish or plate and put it in a warm place – near the fire, for instance – away from any draughts. Cover loosely with foil. (Alternatively, cover it with baking parchment and place a clean, old towel over the top to keep the heat in.) The ideal length of resting time depends on the size of the piece of meat. Sausages and burgers will benefit from 5 minutes or so; meaty ribs, steaks or duck breasts can happily rest for a full 10 minutes; and larger pieces of meat, such as a leg of mutton, need at least 20 minutes' resting.

Barbecuing fish and shellfish

I love cooking fish and shellfish over an open fire. They smell and taste so much better than when they're baked or fried in the kitchen.

Any fish can be cooked over a fire but some, including oily fish such as sardines, sprats, herring and mackerel, are particularly well suited to it. The high oil content of their flesh makes them a little more robust and easier to handle than most white fish, and their bold flavour is beautifully enhanced by the smoky taste you get with open-fire cooking.

Bass and bream cook well over an open fire. Their dense, white, relatively firm flesh makes them fairly resilient to this form of cooking. Other white fish, including whiting, coley, cod and pollack are more fragile. They have more open-grained muscle that separates easily, even in its raw state. They also have thin, delicate skin that tears with ease, so they are not my first choice for open-fire cooking.

Scallops, crab, lobster, mussels, clams, squid and cuttlefish can be cooked over a fire with seriously delicious results. One of my all-time favourite things to do with scallops is to cook them in their own shells in hot embers. The shell acts like a miniature frying pan in which the scallops sizzle away. Salt and pepper and a knob of butter or trickle of olive oil are all you need – though a healthy helping of garlic doesn't go amiss either.

Fish flesh is rather different from meat. The changes in flavour, structure and texture that come about with cooking (protein coagulation, collagen breakdown, caramelisation) all happen at a lower temperature. Fish flesh tends to be cooked through when it reaches a temperature of just 50–55°C – which isn't much hotter than a hot bath. As a result, fish is usually cooked for far less time than meat.

At the risk of repeating myself, heat management is key here. A low, slow heat will cook fish gently and give you more control – but it won't produce the same exciting flavours you get from a higher heat. A brisk blast of heat crisps fish skin, darkens it and gives the flesh depth and character. The goal is to avoid overcooking or drying out the flesh near the surface before the fish is cooked through. The chunkier the fish, the more likely this is to occur. In addition, most fish have a naturally uneven shape, so some areas tend to cook through before others. This is true regardless of whether the fish is whole or filleted.

One way to tackle all these issues is to slash the fish with a sharp knife in its thickest, fleshiest areas before cooking. This helps the heat penetrate the muscle and encourages even cooking. The slashes can also be a way of channelling flavour into the fish as it cooks – both from salt, spices, herbs and oil rubbed in and from the fire's smoke.

To judge whether your fish is cooked, insert the tip of a knife into the flesh and see if it flakes apart. If it does, then it's done. Fish will also lift away from the bone easily when cooked – another way to check it's ready. Test early: if it turns out the fish is not cooked yet, it's an easy fix. Just pop it back over the fire and be patient.

Fish is nowhere near as robust as meat. It won't stand for being chucked around the place, or repeatedly flipped on a grill. It must be handled with care from beginning to end – with an emphasis on end, because that's when it's really prone to breaking up. Taking this into account when you embark on any fish-and-fire journey will make a big difference to the overall results.

Whether you're cooking whole fish (both flat and round) or fillets (either big or small), it's worth oiling the grill, as well as the skin of the fish, before starting. This should, in theory, stop the fish from sticking to the bars. In practice, it doesn't always work – but it's worth doing nonetheless.

Different techniques

I sometimes use an old Aga bread-toaster to cook my fish in (as shown). Essentially, it is just two circular grills hinged together, which I can sandwich smaller whole fish or fish fillets into (see p.94). It's an incredibly practical way to flip the fish (repeatedly) without fear of it breaking up and, since the toaster is hand-held, it's easily moved closer to, or further away from, the heat of the fire. You can also buy purpose-made fish grilling baskets for whole fish.

It's possible to spear a whole fish with a sharpened stick and suspend it near the fire. Insert one end into the fish's mouth to secure it firmly and push the other end in the ground at a 45° angle, and away you go. Alternatively, use metal skewers (two, three or four, depending on the size of the fish) in a similar way. Insert them right through the fish, and support the ends of the skewers on stones or bricks either side of the fire to suspend the fish over the heat. This makes fish easy to turn.

In addition to these classic fish cooking methods, there's nothing to stop you experimenting with new and entertaining ways to cook fish outdoors. It is the spirit of adventure that makes open-fire cooking such fun. You'll find a shoal of wonderful fish and shellfish recipes on pp.90–107, but here's a short list of ideas to whet your appetite:

- **Cover a fish** (scales on) with dry hay. Set light to it. When the hay is burnt through, turn the fish. Repeat until the fish is cooked. For safety, it's best to do this within some kind of fire ring (see p.38).

- **Arrange a few bricks** or large flat stones in the centre of some really hot, glowing embers (see p.28). Lay a bed of fresh herbs such as rosemary, thyme, bay or sage on the stones, then place a fish – or many fish – on top and leave until cooked.

- **Thread some scallops** onto long stems of fresh rosemary, season them with salt and pepper and set over a hot grill. You'll get lovely smoky flavours from the burning rosemary leaves as the scallops cook.

- **Set a pot or metal bucket** of clean seawater on a grill over hot embers (as you do on p.106). When the water is hot (between 65°C and 90°C), drop in a whole fish and poach until cooked.

- **Nail crocodile clips** to a long, strong stick at even intervals. Suspend the stick horizontally above hot embers in the same way you would a basic spit (see pp.76–8). Clip some whole fish or large fillets in place and cook.

- **Give each person** a few sprats or whelks and a sharp stick on which to impale them, and then toast them, like marshmallows.

- **Season a whole fish** with salt and pepper and stuff some herbs and lemon slices into the cavity. Wrap it in several layers of foil and place in the glowing embers of a fire. Turn several times during cooking.

- **Nail a fillet of fish** to a pre-soaked hardwood plank (as shown on p.50) and prop it in the embers of the fire (see p.93).

Barbecuing vegetables and fruit

Outdoor cooking is most often associated with the hiss and smoke of caramelising meat, or the crackle of blistering fish skin – and very wonderful those things are. But some of the most delicious fire-cooked food I've ever enjoyed has come from the plant kingdom.

Cooking vegetables and fruit over an open fire can do extraordinarily good things to them and I think every outdoor cook should give it a try. If you choose to forget about plants, you'll be leaving a huge and exciting area of open-fire cooking unexplored.

The natural sugars in veg and fruit caramelise in the heat of an open fire in the most irresistible way. Add smoke to the equation and the flavour is transformed. I'd go so far as to say that no one should ever write off a particular vegetable until they have tried it barbecued. Plain, boiled beetroot is one thing, for example, but eat it char-striped and smoky from the grill, trickled with a lovely, garlicky dressing and it's a completely different proposition. The same goes for so many vegetables.

And grilling, griddling or roasting are absolutely brilliant treatments for bland or under-ripe fruit, turning it from disappointing to delicious in minutes.

On the fire

One of the great things about cooking fruit and veg over a fire is that it's quite hard to go wrong. If you undercook sausages or chicken, things could get ugly – but under-do your courgettes, your spring onions or your peaches and it barely matters. In fact, since many vegetables taste good raw in any case, I'd argue you couldn't really undercook them – all the different degrees of 'cookedness' are delicious in their own way.

In general you can be pretty relaxed about heat management when cooking fruit and veg. As long as your fire is fairly hot, it will cook. However, it is worth bearing in mind that while most meat and fish reacts in a similar way to the heat of the fire, with the plant kingdom you are dealing with a diverse array of ingredients with quite different characteristics. Fennel will soften and caramelise but needs a bit of time to do so, whereas ripe tomatoes will collapse almost straight away in their own sweet bubbling juices. Courgettes and peppers will wilt quite evenly, while onions or leeks blacken quickly on the outside, leaving a starkly contrasting pale, steamed core within. Just play around a bit, try out a few recipes, and you'll soon get a feel for things.

A common characteristic of plants is that they contain a lot of water but little or no natural fat. So while you don't have to worry about the spitting and flare-ups you can get with meat cooking, you do have to watch what all that juice is doing. Some plants, including courgettes, aubergines, peppers, chillies, asparagus, fennel,

onions, lettuce, chicory and cabbage keep their juices mostly locked up inside and work brilliantly on an open grill. More juicy ingredients, such as mushrooms, plums and peaches, are often best cooked on a flat griddle or frying pan, rather than an open grill, in order to contain their amazingly tasty juices.

Preparing to cook

I don't bother too much with marinades or spice rubs for vegetables. Before cooking, I usually just brush them lightly with a little oil (olive or rapeseed), and sprinkle on plenty of salt and pepper. That's all you need at this stage. After they're cooked, tender and char-striped, you can go to town with fresh herbs, dressings and seasonings. Some veg, including spring onions and sweetcorn cobs in their husks, don't even need pre-oiling because they have their own handy protective wrapping. You can blacken these to your heart's content, knowing that inside the veg will be steamed, tender and glorious.

A lot of veg and fruit is best cut into slices or wedges for grilling or griddling, so there's maximum surface area for caramelisation. Plants are also less dense than meat or fish, and can shrink a lot during cooking so, in general, they take up more grill space than meat – to start with at least. If you don't have a large grill or griddle, you may need to cook your veg in batches. But this is no bad thing because it gives you the opportunity to let it marinate in a dressing after it's come off the heat, soaking up flavour. And, like almost any cooked food, veg is often better after a bit of a 'rest' before serving anyway. Veg and fruit cook more quickly than meat so doing a couple of batches needn't take too long.

Using barbecued fruit and veg

Whereas a piece of fire-cooked meat or fish is often served pretty much as it comes, the joy of grilled veg and fruit is that it can be built into multi-layered dishes. I love tossing grilled veg with leaves, nuts, seeds and cheese to make amazing salads, for example, or putting several different types of veg in a bap or pitta bread, with some dressing and sauce – and perhaps meat too, or maybe not.

The best thing to do is experiment – feel free to try cooking almost any edible plant over an open fire. Brussels sprouts, cauliflower, broad beans and peas (in the pod) all work well. The worst thing that can happen is that things get a little burnt. And actually there's every chance you'll discover a whole new world of smoky, fired-up, plant-based deliciousness.

Indispensable kit

Although I'm not a huge fan of kit, there are some basics that any keen open-fire cook should have to hand. None of the equipment I use is particularly expensive and some of the most useful items in my fire-cooking toolbox are things I've just happened to come across over the years. I suggest browsing in charity shops or car boot sales from time to time; these are great places for you to find useful stuff.

- **A stout wooden stick** For poking, prodding, riddling and other manoeuvres. Wooden sticks used as fire tools have a limited life-span, of course, but are generally easily replaced…

- **A couple of pairs of tongs** For lifting things on and off the fire. I have one large, hefty pair for moving hot bricks or stones.

- **A sharp pocket knife** An essential tool for every outdoor cook.

- **Grills of mixed sizes** These needn't be specifically designed for outdoor cooking: I'm a fan of old wire cooling racks, Aga bread-toasters and oven racks.

- **A stiff wire brush** You'll find this useful for scrubbing your grill before cooking and generally keeping stuff clean.

- **Butcher's hooks** Brilliant, indestructible things, I use butcher's hooks for hanging meat – or anything else for that matter – over a fire.

- **Splitting axe** Essential for splitting logs.

- **Hatchet** For cutting branches and kindling.

- **Cast-iron pots and pans** For cooking in embers or frying over the fire. I particularly recommend a Dutch oven or a South African potjie pot, both of which have legs that make them practical for open-fire cooking.

- **Digital probe thermometer** Very useful for determining the precise internal 'core' temperature of the food you are cooking.

- **Fireproof gloves** For obvious reasons.

Lamb in spiced yoghurt
with toasted fenugreek and lemon

Many of the spices associated with Indian cookery have a natural affinity with fire and smoke. Cumin and fenugreek are no exception, as this lovely, simple recipe demonstrates. The natural acidity of yoghurt has a mildly tenderising effect – so the longer you leave the lamb to marinate, the more tender it will be. The yoghurt also carries flavour and helps to keep the meat moist as it cooks.

I made this little fire in an old piece of circular steel I found lying around at River Cottage. I'm not sure what it was originally – a piece of farm machinery perhaps – but it worked perfectly, both containing the fire and radiating its heat.

Serves 2

75ml natural wholemilk sheep's or cow's yoghurt
1 large garlic clove, peeled and finely grated
Grated zest and juice of ½ lemon
1 tsp ground fenugreek, toasted

1 tsp ground cumin
½ tsp ground turmeric
2 large lamb leg steaks, about 150g each and 3–4cm thick
Sea salt and freshly ground black pepper

To prepare the marinade, mix together the yoghurt, garlic, lemon zest and juice, and the ground spices. Season to taste with salt and pepper.

Massage the yoghurt mixture into the lamb steaks and lay them in a shallow dish. Cover and place in the fridge to marinate. You can do this several hours ahead or even the day before, but it's also fine to do it just an hour or so before cooking.

Prepare your fire (see pp.26–30). You want lovely hot glowing embers so the lamb will cook fairly quickly.

When the fire is ready, set a grill over it; it's at the right temperature when you can hover your hand above it for a maximum of 2 seconds. Place the lamb steaks on the grill and cook for 3–4 minutes on each side, depending on the heat of your fire, until nicely golden. If you cut the meat open, it should be just a little pink on the inside. This way it will be lovely and juicy.

Transfer the lamb to a warm plate and leave to rest for a few minutes before slicing it thickly. Sprinkle with a little more sea salt and serve with flatbreads (p.136) or pitta breads, a well-dressed green salad and maybe a little fruity chutney.

Fire-roast pork belly
with thyme

If you have good free-range or organic pork, the simplest treatments – like this one – are often the most delicious. Pork belly is usually considered a 'low and slow' cut and is often cooked for hours in a low oven. But because they are cut thinly, these slender slices of pork belly cook relatively quickly over a hot fire and are nice and tender to eat.

The old animal trough pictured here holds a fire brilliantly. The rusty holes in its base allow air to be drawn up into the fire, and the long slender shape makes it possible to cook several ingredients at different temperatures simultaneously: the heat across the base will range from hot-ish at the sides to super-hot in the middle.

Serves 2

4 strips of free-range or organic pork belly, about 2cm thick, skin on if possible
1 tbsp olive oil

3–4 sprigs of thyme
Sea salt and freshly ground black pepper

First prepare your fire (see pp.26–30). You should be cooking over a bed of glowing embers and the heat should be moderate, to avoid the pork fat flaring too much.

When the fire is ready, set a grill over it; it's at the right temperature when you can hover your hand above it for a maximum of 4 seconds. Season the strips of pork belly generously on both sides with salt and pepper then trickle with olive oil and tear over the thyme leaves.

Place the meat on the grill and cook for about 10 minutes. Keep a close eye on it: you'll need to turn the strips regularly to ensure the pork turns nice and golden without burning. Rest the pork for a few moments to one side of the heat. Eat the belly strips hot from the grill – they're pretty fabulous served on their own.

Goat and fig kebabs

These simple kebabs always remind me of Greece, or perhaps some other Mediterranean place that's equally beautiful and romantic. I can almost touch the parched earth, smell the heady scent from the fig trees in the morning, and hear the bleating of young goats as… okay, we'll stop there.

You can prepare the same recipe with lamb or hogget.

Serves 4

400g boneless goat kid leg, trimmed and cut into large cubes
1 small red onion, peeled and finely diced
1 garlic clove, peeled and crushed to a paste
A handful of thyme sprigs, leaves picked

Grated zest of ½ lemon
2 tbsp extra virgin olive oil
6 ripe figs, quartered
1–2 tbsp flaked almonds, toasted
1 tbsp runny honey
Sea salt and freshly ground black pepper

Place the cubed meat in a bowl with the red onion, garlic, thyme leaves and lemon zest. Spoon over the extra virgin olive oil and turn the meat to coat. Place in the fridge to marinate for 2–3 hours, or overnight.

To assemble the kebabs, thread the goat and fig pieces alternately onto kebab sticks; 3 or 4 pieces of each should make a good-sized kebab. Season generously with salt and pepper.

Prepare your fire (see pp.26–30). You want lovely hot embers so the kebabs will cook fairly quickly.

When the fire is ready, set a grill over it; it's reached the right temperature when you can hover your hand above the grill for a maximum of 2 seconds. Lay the kebabs on the grill and cook for 4–5 minutes on each side, keeping a close eye on them and not letting them burn.

Allow the kebabs to rest somewhere warm for 5 minutes before scattering over the flaked almonds and trickling on a little honey. Serve with flatbreads (p.136), hummus, pickled chillies and yoghurt.

P.S. If using wooden skewers, pre-soak them in water for 30 minutes to help stop them catching and burning on the grill.

Fire-bricked steaks

Hot stones or fire bricks (see p.155) are such fun to cook with. Placed in a fire, they soak up heat like sponges and hold it inside. They can be glowing hot but still transfer an even, radial heat to the food you place on them – unlike metal, which conducts heat in a far more aggressive way. As steak like this should be served rare, it won't take much time to cook. This is real fast food.

Serves 2–4

About 500g sirloin or ribeye steak, about 2cm thick
1 tbsp olive oil
Sea salt and freshly ground black pepper

You will also need
4 fire bricks

Prepare a good fire (see pp.26–30), one with a large hot heart.

Place the fire bricks in the heart of the fire to heat up. Keep feeding the fire with dry wood to achieve the maximum transfer of heat. The bricks will take at least half an hour to get up to temperature. When they are ludicrously hot (almost glowing), carefully lift out two of the bricks and place them, side by side, on the ground.

Season the steak with salt and pepper and rub with the olive oil. Lay the steak on top of the bricks. It should start to sizzle. Use a pair of heavy kitchen or fire tongs to take the remaining two bricks and put them on top of the steak. Leave to cook for 1–2 minutes.

Remove the steak from the bricks and let it rest for 4–5 minutes before slicing. Served in buttered baguettes with fried onions and mustard, it is absolutely perfect.

Clay-baked venison
with juniper and hay

Encasing food in clay and baking it in the embers of the fire is a technique that goes back many thousands of years. The clay forms a barrier between the food and the direct heat of the fire, meaning delicate ingredients like fish and lean meat such as venison can be cooked very successfully.

Clay has good insulating qualities; it also conducts heat evenly and consistently, dissipating any hot spots. This is great news for open-fire cooking, because there will always be some areas of a fire that are hotter or cooler than others. What's more, clay keeps in moisture so the food inside it is effectively steamed, which helps it to stay incredibly moist. Natural potter's clay is available from specialist suppliers (see Directory, p.248).

Serves 2

750g wild venison loin
1 tbsp olive oil
14–18 juniper berries, crushed
4 bay leaves, thinly sliced into ribbons
1 tsp chopped thyme leaves
Sea salt and freshly ground black pepper

You will also need
2kg natural potter's clay
½ bucket of clean, dry hay

Prepare a hot fire (see pp.26–30).

Place the venison loin on a board or tray and use a sharp knife to trim away any membrane or sinew. Trickle the olive oil over the meat and rub it in. Sprinkle over the crushed juniper, ribboned bay, thyme and a generous amount of salt and pepper and massage into the meat (pic 1).

Divide the clay in half. Roll and pat each piece out on a sheet of baking parchment to roughly the same shape as the piece of venison (pic 2), 1.5–2cm thick and 3–4cm bigger all round, so you will have a margin of clay that you can seal together.

Lay a small bed of hay in the centre of one of the sheets of clay. Set the meat down on the hay (pic 3). Take some more hay and lay it over the top, encasing the meat. Try not to let the hay spill out over the margin or you'll have difficulty sealing the two halves together.

Lay the second piece of clay over the hay and meat (pic 4). Bring up the edges of the bottom sheet of clay and crimp them together with the edges of the top sheet, sealing well and smoothing out the seams so that the steam will stay locked in

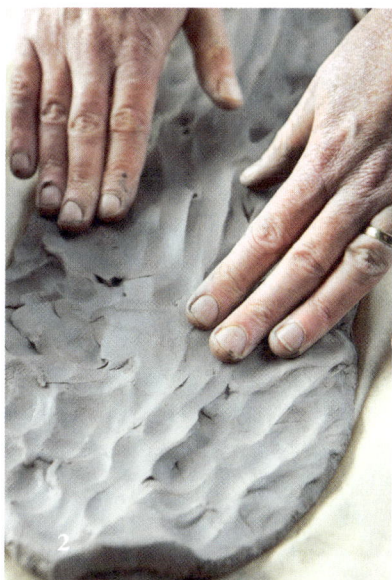

when the meat is cooking. Your fire should be really nice and hot by now with smaller glowing embers and slightly larger, charred, flaming pieces of wood.

Clear some of the larger embers away from the centre of the fire. Level out the ember bed then carefully lift the clay parcel off the parchment and lay it down on the embers. Use some tongs to lift some of the larger glowing embers and arrange them over the top and around the clay so as to get heat travelling into it from all sides. Cook for 25–30 minutes.

Lift the hot embers away from the clay-wrapped venison and clear a space around it (pic 5), then use a spade or peel to lift the clay parcel from the fire and set it down on a board or the ground.

Use the back of a knife or a sharp pair of tongs to break the clay into pieces (pic 6). Lift these away – be careful, as they will be hot. Brush the hay from the meat and lift it out onto a board.

Allow the meat to rest somewhere warm for 5 minutes before cutting it into thick slices and serving. This is very good with green beans or broccoli dressed with olive oil and orange (or lemon) zest and juice.

Campfire rabbit
with bacon, cider and herbs

Anything you might cook in a pan on the stove indoors can also be cooked outside on an open fire, as long as you don't mind the underside of your pan getting a bit dark. You can easily shift the pan around to make the most of hotter or cooler areas of the fire. Although the rabbit isn't in direct contact with the fire, it takes on flavour as the smoke rises up and curls over the pan.

Serves 2–4

400g piece smoked bacon, cut into
    2–3cm chunks, or 400g lardons
1 wild rabbit, jointed into 6 pieces
1 large onion, peeled and sliced
4 garlic cloves, peeled and sliced
6 bay leaves

10 sage leaves
2 sprigs of rosemary
500ml medium cider
Up to 300ml water
Sea salt and freshly ground
    black pepper

Prepare your fire (see pp.26–30). You are looking to achieve a consistent, gentle heat. Set a grill over the fire once it has died back to glowing embers, and put a sturdy, thick-bottomed flameproof pot on top (or nestle it directly in the embers).

When you can hover your hand above the grill for a maximum of 3 seconds, and the pot is hot, add the bacon. Stir it around in the pot as it starts to render some of its fat and keep frying until it is a lovely golden brown colour, then transfer it to a large bowl using a slotted spoon, leaving the fat in the pan.

Season the jointed rabbit with salt and pepper and add to the pan. Brown the rabbit on all sides then remove with a slotted spoon and set aside with the bacon.

Toss the onion and garlic into the fat remaining in the pan, along with the herbs and plenty of salt and pepper, and cook for 5–10 minutes, until soft.

Return the rabbit and bacon to the pan, pour in the cider and top up with enough water to just cover the meat. Get some heat under the pot so it comes to a simmer then cook, with the lid slightly ajar, for 2–3 hours. During this time you'll need to keep the fire ticking over. If the stew stops simmering the fire will need fuel, so lift the pot off, raise the grill and add more wood. You may also have to top up the pan with a little water to ensure the rabbit and bacon stay covered.

The rabbit is ready when it is so tender it falls away from the bone. Take the pot off the fire and taste to check the seasoning. Serve with good bread.

Homemade beef burgers
with bacon and cheese

Beef burgers are easy to knock up and always so much better than anything you can buy. These burgers are made with skirt steak, a flavoursome open-grained cut. I like to mince the steak with some beef fat or suet to give it extra moisture and a richer, beefier flavour. A crank-handled mincer works well – you see them at car boot sales all the time. If you don't have a mincer, ask the butcher to mince the mix for you or, if push comes to shove, chop the meat and fat in a food processor.

Get the fire really hot so that the bars of the grill char the burgers. This gives them character; it also helps to cook them fast and keeps them juicy. I serve them in buns with streaky bacon and Cheddar – the perfect partners in crime.

Makes 4

400g skirt steak
100g fresh beef suet or beef fat
1 tbsp chopped thyme leaves
1 heaped tsp fine sea salt
Freshly ground black pepper

To assemble

About 150g good Cheddar
Pickled cucumbers or gherkins
8 rashers of streaky bacon
4 soft burger buns, lightly toasted

Mince the skirt steak and suet or fat together (see above), place in a large bowl and season with the thyme, salt and plenty of pepper. Use clean hands to mix the meat and seasonings thoroughly and bind the mixture together. Divide the seasoned beef into 4 portions and shape into burgers, each about 125g and no thicker than 2cm.

Slice the cheese and pickled cucumbers thinly. When everything is ready to go, get your fire going (see pp.26–30); you want a good deep bed of really hot embers. Set a grill over the fire.

Once everything is glowing super-hot, and you can hover your hand above the grill for 1 second at most, lay the burgers carefully on the grill. They should start to sizzle and smoke immediately. Cook for 2–3 minutes on each side. I like to serve the burgers just under medium but you can leave them on a minute or two longer. You need a searing heat, to ensure the burgers take on lots of colour and stay juicy.

A minute or so after turning the burgers, add the bacon to the grill. (At this point you should be able to hover your hand above the grill for a maximum of 4 seconds.) Cook until crisp on both sides. When the burgers are almost done, lay the cheese slices on top and let them melt. (Move the bacon to one side if it's done.) Pop the burgers into the buns with the bacon rashers and pickled cucumbers and serve.

Mutton with wild garlic
and seaweed butter

I think you might find that salty, smoky mutton cooked over a glowing open fire is one of the most delicious things you'll ever eat. I love mutton – it's got spades of flavour. In most cases, this meat comes from sheep that have been able to follow their natural grazing habits over at least two summers – a much longer and more active life than that of the younger animals sold as lamb meat. Leg of mutton is dark and marbled with ivory-coloured fat.

Serves 8–10

1 trimmed, boned-out leg of mutton (or hogget or lamb), about 3–4kg
2 tbsp olive oil
A handful of wild garlic leaves, finely chopped (or 1 garlic clove, peeled and finely chopped)
Sea salt and freshly ground black pepper

For the flavoured butter

50g butter, softened
2 tbsp dried seaweed flakes (I like those from the Cornish Seaweed Company)
A small bunch of wild garlic leaves, finely chopped (or 2–3 garlic cloves, peeled and finely chopped)

For the salsa verde

1 small garlic clove, peeled
A generous bunch of flat-leaf parsley, trimmed of coarse stalks
About 15–20 basil leaves
3–4 sprigs of tarragon, leaves picked
4–5 anchovy fillets in oil
About 1 tsp capers
About 1 tsp Dijon or English mustard
A pinch of sugar
A few drops of lemon juice or wine vinegar
2–3 tbsp extra virgin olive oil
Freshly ground black pepper

You will also need

Heavy cotton string, soaked in cold water, for tying the meat
Several butcher's hooks

First make the flavoured butter: put the softened butter, seaweed flakes and wild garlic (or ordinary garlic) into a bowl and season with plenty of salt and pepper. Mix well.

Open out the mutton and spoon the butter into the bone cavity, making sure it's evenly distributed. Now roll up the leg and secure it with string in several places. If you're familiar with the 'butcher's knot', use it – but any secure knot will work, as long as it doesn't come undone. Pre-soaking the string in water first helps stop it catching alight above the fire.

Season the meat all over with salt and pepper and rub with the olive oil and chopped wild (or ordinary) garlic. Set it aside to come up to ambient temperature while you prepare the fire.

Get your fire going and let it build up (see pp.26–30). The base of the fire should be circular and large enough that when the mutton is hung above it, it will get heat from all sides.

To suspend the meat, I make a simple spit from some lengths of hazel or driftwood: a basic contraption, easily replicated. The frame consists of two uprights with Y-shaped tops that form a sort of crutch for the cross bar section that sits over the fire. It's from this that I will suspend the meat, using a butcher's hook (or two or three linked together to form a short chain). I then adjust the height of the meat during cooking by simply adding or subtracting hooks. I will also turn the meat so that it cooks evenly, by relocating the hook in the meat at regular time intervals.

When the flames have burnt down and you have some really hot embers glowing away, suspend the mutton over the fire. It should be no more than 60cm above the embers, and the temperature should be such that you can't hold your hand beneath the meat for any length of time.

Turn the meat periodically, as well as raising or lowering it, so it cooks consistently. Keep feeding the fire and watching it: be on hand to make small adjustments. Cook the meat until it is piping hot throughout; this will take several hours. I'm being intentionally vague here: there are too many variables involved to suggest exact cooking times. To get an idea of how it's getting on, press a skewer or small knife into the thickest part of the meat, leave it there for 30 seconds then take it out and touch it to your wrist for an instant. If it feels burning hot, the meat will be ready. When the meat is cooked to medium it will register an internal temperature of 60°C or thereabouts on a digital probe thermometer. If you prefer it well done then continue to cook it until it registers 72°C. Either way, take it off the fire and transfer it to a warm dish to rest for 20 minutes.

To make the salsa verde, finely chop the garlic on a board. Add the herbs, anchovies and capers and chop the ingredients together until well mixed and fairly fine in texture. Transfer to a bowl and mix in the mustard, sugar, lemon juice or wine vinegar and pepper, plus enough olive oil to give a glossy, spoonable consistency, tasting and tweaking the mixture as you go. (This sauce is best made immediately before serving but it will keep for a few days in a sealed jar, in the fridge.)

Slice the mutton thickly and serve with the salsa verde, and fire-baked jacket potatoes if you like.

My kind of lamb kofte

Good lamb or hogget has so much flavour, it can handle pungent spices like the ones I've chosen here. These kofte are incredibly easy to make and quick to cook. You could grill them in the kitchen, but they'll taste better cooked over a hot fire. If you're using wooden skewers, remember to pre-soak them (see p.64).

Makes 6

2 tsp cumin seeds
2 tsp fennel seeds
2 tsp black peppercorns
500g minced lamb, hogget or mutton
1 medium-hot red chilli, finely chopped
4 garlic cloves, peeled and grated
2 tsp nigella seeds
Olive oil, for cooking
Sea salt and freshly ground
    black pepper

For the minted yoghurt
¼ cucumber, peeled and cut into
    1cm cubes
A bunch of mint, leaves picked and
    shredded into thin ribbons
½ garlic clove, peeled and finely grated
    or crushed to a paste
4 tbsp natural yoghurt
1 tbsp olive oil

Set a small pan over the fire (or the kitchen hob). Add the cumin and fennel seeds along with the peppercorns and toast gently for 3–4 minutes. Tip the contents of the pan into a mortar and grind the spices with a pestle to a fairly fine texture.

Put the minced meat into a large bowl. Add the ground spices, chilli, garlic, nigella seeds and some salt and pepper. Use clean hands to mix the meat and seasonings thoroughly and bind the mixture together. Flour your hands lightly and divide the mixture into 6 portions. Mould into long sausage shapes and thread onto skewers, then place in the fridge to chill and firm up for at least an hour.

For the minted yoghurt, place the cucumber, mint, garlic, yoghurt and olive oil in a bowl, add some salt and pepper and gently turn it all together. Set aside.

When you're ready, light the fire (see pp.26–30). You want a bed of hot embers for this, as the lamb is quite fatty and might flare up if the fire is flaming. Set a grill over the embers; it's reached the right temperature when you can hover your hand above the grill for a maximum of 2 seconds.

Brush the kofte with a little oil and place on the grill. Cook for 10–12 minutes, turning occasionally, until golden brown all over and cooked through. Serve with the minted yoghurt and flatbreads (p.136), as well as some fresh coriander leaves, jalapeños and a scattering of fennel fronds, if you have some.

Wild venison stew
with pearled barley

When you're outdoors and you've got a fire going, it feels right to cook meat from an animal that's had a truly wild life, like venison. Sometimes I add bacon or pancetta to venison stew because the fat helps keep everything rich and moist, but here you can achieve a similar effect using pearled barley. It has a gelatinous, starchy quality, not to mention a gorgeous nutty texture.

Serves 3–4

1 tbsp olive oil or lard
500g boneless venison shoulder, cubed
1 large or 2 smaller onions, peeled
    and sliced
4 garlic cloves, peeled and
    thinly sliced

2 sprigs of rosemary
2 bay leaves
1 litre good chicken, game or veg stock
50g pearled barley, well rinsed
Sea salt and freshly ground
    black pepper

Prepare your fire (see pp.26–30). Let it burn until you have a bed of hot embers with an occasional flame.

When the fire is ready, set a grill over it and position your large casserole dish on the grill; if you're using a heavy cast-iron pot or Dutch oven you can place it straight onto the hot embers.

Add the olive oil or lard to your cooking pot, followed by the cubed venison – it should sizzle; if it doesn't, move the dish to a hotter part of the fire or add more fuel. Season the meat with salt and pepper and fry on all sides for 4–5 minutes, until it's beginning to colour. Add the onion, garlic and herbs and continue to cook, stirring, for 8–10 minutes.

Pour over the stock and bring to a gentle simmer. Cook the stew, with the lid set slightly ajar, at a very low, tremulous simmer for about 1½ hours.

Now add the rinsed pearled barley and simmer for a further 40 minutes. If the stew looks a little dry at any point, then add a dash of water. When the meat is lovely and tender, taste the liquor and adjust the seasoning.

Remove the pan from the heat and allow it to sit for 15 minutes before serving. This is great with some warm flatbreads (p.136) for mopping up the juices.

Ember-cooked steak

Placing a lovely looking piece of steak straight in the fire will, to some, appear quite mad, but fear not. The flavour you achieve when you cook directly in embers is incredible and the meat won't burn, because the moment you lay it on top of the glowing coals, it cuts off their oxygen and the cooking temperature reduces almost immediately. Still, don't turn your back on it!

Serves 2

1 large skirt steak, trimmed, about
    500g and 2–3cm thick
A trickle of olive oil
Flaky sea salt and freshly ground
    black pepper

Light your fire (see pp.26–30). Let it burn until you have a bed of chunky, white, glowing embers; charcoal works well here.

When you are ready to cook, blow or fan away the excess ash from the embers. Rub the steak with the olive oil and season with salt and pepper. Lay the steak on top of the embers and cook for 2–2½ minutes on each side.

To judge 'doneness', press the steak with your finger and see how much give it has. If it feels fairly soft, that means it's still quite rare. Medium-rare is better for skirt steak – you want it to feel not firm but not too soft.

Transfer the steak from the embers to a serving dish using tongs. If there are any rogue embers clinging to the steak's surface, remove these and scrape away any excess ash. Rest the steak by the fire for 5–10 minutes before slicing. If you find that the steak isn't cooked to your liking, throw it back in the fire for a few more minutes, rest it again, then have another go. Season the slices of steak with a little flaky salt and serve.

Lamb ribs with fennel,
garlic and lemon

There's something irresistible about the combination of sizzling lamb fat, heat and smoke. Here I prefer to use long, meaty (and fatty) ribs cut from the breast of a hogget (a sheep in its second year). But you could use the ribs from a slightly younger animal; pork ribs work well too. The ribs are teamed with lemon to cut through their richness, and fennel which adds its own sweetness. I also use fennel stalks and fronds if I have them, to perfume the smoke.

Serves 4

1.5kg hogget or lamb ribs, cut long
    from the thick end
2 tbsp olive oil
1 tbsp fennel seeds, lightly crushed
Grated zest and juice of 1 large
    lemon

A good pinch of dried chilli flakes
Fresh fennel stalks and fronds from
    the top of the bulb (if available)
2–3 garlic cloves, peeled and sliced
Flaky sea salt and freshly ground
    black pepper

Light your fire (see pp.26–30). You're looking for a medium-hot bed of glowing embers that give off a nice even heat.

Set a grill over the embers – I like to use one that I can lift off quickly, so I can easily deal with any flare-ups from the dripping fat. You're ready to cook when you can hover your hand above the grill for a maximum of 4 seconds.

Place the ribs on a large tray. Mix 1 tbsp olive oil with the crushed fennel seeds, lemon zest, chilli flakes and plenty of salt and pepper. Rub all over the ribs to coat.

Place the ribs on the grill over the fire. Cook, turning regularly, for 15–20 minutes until lovely and brown, and looking delicious. Then, if you have some fennel stalks, lift the ribs off and cover the grill with them. Return the ribs to the grill and cook over the smoking fennel for another 10 minutes or so. (If you don't have fennel stalks then simply cook the ribs for a further 10 minutes anyway.)

Remove the ribs to a clean tray and rest near the fire. Brush the fennel stalks aside (into the fire) and place a small pan on the grill. Add the remaining 1 tbsp olive oil followed by the garlic. Allow to sizzle for 30–40 seconds, but don't let it burn.

Pour the garlicky oil over the ribs. Add the fennel tops and lemon juice and tumble together. Season with a little flaky salt and serve at once, with napkins.

Grilled duck breasts
with rosemary and garlic

The first time I grilled duck breasts on an open fire was at the height of summer, in a beautiful old walled garden in southern France. We had managed to get hold of the duck breasts from a local farm and cooked them that evening under the fig tree with the hum of cicadas around us. It's a powerful memory that comes back to me every time I cook this dish.

I keep the fire gentle here – a bed of slow-glowing embers is all you need. This gives the duck fat time to soften and render, resulting in deliciously crisp skin.

Serves 3–4

2 free-range duck breasts, about
    350g each
1 whole garlic bulb, halved around
    its 'equator'

6 sprigs of rosemary
Sea salt and freshly ground
    black pepper

Prepare your fire; it doesn't need to be big or particularly voracious (see pp.26–30).

Place the duck breasts on a board, skin side up. Use a very sharp knife to score shallow, criss-cross cuts in the duck skin, about 1cm apart, going through the skin and down into the fat. Season the skin with fine salt.

When the fire is glowing gently, set a grill over it. The temperature is right when you can hover your hand above the grill for a maximum of 5 seconds. Place the duck breasts, skin side down, on the grill. Nestle the garlic and rosemary next to them and season the surface of the duck breasts with salt and pepper.

Cook the duck breasts for 25–30 minutes. This relatively long, gentle cooking softens the fat and colours and crisps the skin. If the fat drips and causes the fire to flare up, dampen the flames with a spray of water, or remove the meat from the grill until the flames have settled. You don't want flames scorching the skin of the duck.

Turn the duck breasts over and cook for a further 10–15 minutes on the flesh side. I cook them medium-rare, aiming for an internal temperature of about 55°C on a digital probe thermometer. If you prefer them more well done, aim for 60°C. Once cooked to your liking, remove the duck breasts from the grill and leave them to rest somewhere warm for 10–15 minutes.

Slice the duck breasts thickly and serve with the soft grilled garlic, a green salad, new potatoes and bread.

Fire-roast mackerel
with tomatoes and aubergine purée

Mackerel has to be my favourite fish for cooking outside over an open fire. Its skin crisps beautifully while underneath the oily flesh stays moist and tender. The fresher the mackerel, the more delicate and delicious its flavour will be, so select fish with nice bright eyes and vibrant, colourful skin. Ripe, sweet tomatoes and a garlicky bashed aubergine purée make this a great summer's night dish.

Serves 4

4 good-sized, super-fresh mackerel,
    gutted and cleaned
2 tbsp olive oil
8 small sprigs of rosemary
250g large, ripe tomatoes, halved
Sea salt and freshly ground
    black pepper

For the aubergine purée
2 medium aubergines
2 garlic cloves, peeled and grated
1 tbsp tahini
A pinch of dried chilli flakes
A handful of basil leaves, chopped
2 tbsp extra virgin olive oil

Prepare your fire (see pp.26–30); you want to be cooking over glowing embers.

When the fire is hot, set a grill over it, making sure it's clean so your fish is less likely to stick to the bars. You'll know the temperature is right when you can hover your hand above the grill for a maximum of 3 seconds.

Lay the fish on a board and, using a sharp knife, cut several shallow slash marks on both sides. Trickle the olive oil over the fish, sprinkle with salt and pepper and rub in, getting right into the slash marks. Place a couple of rosemary sprigs in each fish cavity. Set the fish on the grill. Season the tomatoes with salt and pepper and place, cut side up, next to the fish. Place the aubergines (uncut) on the grill too.

Turn the aubergines every few minutes, to ensure they cook evenly. The fish will take 6–8 minutes on each side, depending on size. Don't worry if the skin tears; the fish will still taste amazing. Once the mackerel are cooked, remove them from the grill and keep warm. Turn the tomatoes after 10–15 minutes and keep cooking them until they are soft and caramelised, then remove to a plate.

When the aubergines are soft (this will take about 20 minutes), slit open and scoop the soft flesh out into a bowl. Add the garlic, tahini, chilli flakes, basil, extra virgin olive oil and some salt and pepper. Mix and mash the aubergine with the seasonings.

Divide the aubergine purée between 4 plates. Add the tomatoes and fish and serve.

'Planked' fish

This traditional Scandinavian way of cooking involves fixing fillets of fish to a hardwood plank and settling it in the embers of a hot fire. Sometimes the foot of the board begins to smoulder and smoke, which gives the fish an incredible flavour.

The process is a little mad, but it gives delicious results. There's nothing to it, either: you just need a decent piece of hardwood. Cedar is traditional, but I've found that oak, beech and alder work really well, too. You'll also need a large fillet of fresh fish (skin on), such as cod, pollack or sea trout, some nails and a hammer.

Serves up to 4

A bunch of woody herbs (bay, fennel
    stalks, parsley, juniper etc.)
1 lemon, sliced
1 fish fillet, at least 500g and up to 2kg
A little olive oil, or softened butter
Sea salt and freshly ground
    black pepper

You will also need
A plank of hardwood, about
    50 x 30 x 5cm (see above)

Planking fish like this is particularly suited to a camp fire (i.e. an open fire on the ground) but it can be done on a conventional barbecue too. The fire needs to be hot embers and gently smoking wood; the odd flame is fine. Soak the plank in some fresh water for an hour or so; this will stop it catching in the heat of the fire. It's good if it smoulders, but not if it erupts in flames.

Place the soaked plank on the ground and arrange the herbs and lemon slices down the centre. Lay the fish, skin side down, on top, rub it with olive oil or butter and season well with salt and pepper. Secure the fish in place with 4 or 5 steel nails.

You're going to set the plank upright in the embers, so clear away the burning wood from a small semi-circular area, downwind of the hottest and flamiest part of the fire, so that any breeze will carry the heat and smoke towards the fish.

Using a log, carefully prop up the plank in the fire, in the cleared area. The fish should be on the upward-facing side of the plank, with the thickest part of the fillet nearest the ground. Leave it to cook gently for about 25–30 minutes. The base of the plank may start to smoulder; if it ignites, extinguish it with a splash of water.

When the fish is cooked, lift the plank out of the fire and set it directly on the table (you might want to douse the scorched base in water first). Let everyone dig in then and there. Good bread, lemon juice and mayonnaise are all you need alongside.

Campfire roast fish fillets
with burnt lemon and thyme

For this super-easy recipe, you'll need a wire bread-toaster or some other form of grill basket – it needs to be shallow, so that it holds the fish fillets and lemon snugly. I use an old Aga toaster – you sometimes see them in junk shops or on sale for a snip at car boot sales. Grab one if you can. Mine has been indispensable, although I've never actually used it for toast…

Serves 4

2 medium lemons, thinly sliced
A large bunch of thyme
4 large wild bream fillets
A pinch of dried chilli flakes

2 tbsp olive oil
Sea salt and freshly ground
    black pepper

Prepare your fire – you're going to need a bed of hot embers (see pp.26–30).

Open out the bread-toaster or grill basket and lay the lemon slices over one half of it in a single layer. Scatter the thyme over the lemons.

Season the fish fillets with plenty of salt and pepper and rub them with the chilli flakes and olive oil. Place them skin side down on the thyme. Close the basket and set it, lemon side down, over the hot fire.

Cook for 6–8 minutes, until the lemons are charred and blackening, then carefully flip the basket over and cook the fish on the other side for another couple of minutes, or until it is just done.

Open the basket and lift the fish onto plates. Add a few pieces of lemon to each plate – it will be soft and bitter-sweet. Serve with buttered new potatoes.

Newspaper-wrapped bream
(or other whole fish)

This is a brilliant way to cook fish in the embers of a fire. Wrapped up in a wet newspaper parcel, the fish steams gently and stays beautifully moist. You won't get crisp skin, but if you use lots of herbs the flesh will be delightfully aromatic.

Serves 2–4

2 black bream, trout or large mackerel, cleaned
A few knobs of butter, softened
1 lemon, thinly sliced, plus wedges for serving
A handful of bay leaves

A bunch of bushy, tender thyme
4 sprigs of rosemary
4 garlic cloves
Sea salt and freshly ground black pepper

Prepare your fire (see pp.26–30); you're going to need a bed of hot embers.

Lay two sheets of newspaper side by side on your work surface and cover each with another sheet. (Add an extra sheet to each pile if you're using a tabloid rather than a broadsheet.)

Rub the fish with the softened butter and season them well with salt and pepper. Arrange some of the lemon slices in the middle of each pile of newspaper and scatter over some of the bay leaves, thyme and rosemary. Place the seasoned fish on top. Bash the garlic cloves and pop them into the fish cavities, then surround the fish with the remaining lemon slices and herbs.

Wrap each fish in the newspaper, tucking in the ends so you have nice, sealed, snug-looking parcels. Soak each parcel in fresh water until the paper is wet through.

Clear some of the bigger embers from the middle of the fire with a stick and place the wet parcels in the space. Cook for 15–20 minutes, turning them occasionally so they cook evenly, until the paper is charred and starting to catch fire (if it catches fire sooner than this, sprinkle or spray with water).

Unwrap the fish carefully, lift away the herbs, and serve with lemon wedges, a salad and some bread and butter.

Clay-baked trout
with lemon and dill

Sometimes cooking fish on a fire can be a little problematic: it's a fragile ingredient and becomes more so when cooked. However, encasing it in clay protects it from the high heat of the fire, holds it together and keeps it moist and delicious. Clay-baking is also great fun, culminating in a 'reveal' when you break away the baked casing. Kids love it.

Serves 4

1 large brown or rainbow trout,
    750g–1kg, gutted
A large bunch of dill
1 lemon, ½ sliced and ½ for squeezing
1 shallot, peeled and thinly sliced
Sea salt and freshly ground
    black pepper

You will also need
About 2–3kg natural potter's clay

Prepare your fire (see pp.26–30); you'll want it to be made up of glowing embers and slightly larger charred flaming pieces of hardwood.

Rinse and dry the fish but leave the scales in place.

Divide the clay in half. Roll each piece out on a sheet of baking parchment, forming it into a roughly fish-shaped piece, 1.5–2cm thick and 3–4cm bigger all around than your actual fish.

Lay about half the dill over the centre of one of the clay sheets. Place a few slices of lemon on top and scatter over half the shallot slices. Lay the fish on top. Place the remaining lemon slices over the fish, followed by the rest of the shallot slices.

Cover the fish as evenly as possible with the remaining dill, encasing the fish in a fragrant natural envelope. Be careful not to let any of the ingredients spill out onto the clay margin around the fish or you'll have difficulty sealing the clay together.

Lay the second piece of clay over the trout. Bring up the edges of the clay and crimp them really well together, sealing and smoothing out the seams so that the steam will stay locked in when the fish is cooking.

When the fire is ready, clear some of the larger embers away from the centre with a stick. Level out the ember bed then carefully lift the clay parcel off the parchment and lay it down on the bed.

Use tongs to lift some of the larger hot embers and arrange them over the top and around the clay, to get heat travelling in from all sides. Cook for 25–30 minutes.

Lift the hot embers away from the cooked clay-wrapped trout and clear a space around it, then use a spade or something similar to lift the clay parcel from the fire and set it down on a board or the ground.

Carefully break the clay shell with the back of a heavy knife and lift the hot pieces away with tongs. Remove the dill and lemon from the surface of the fish then carefully lift the scaly skin away to reveal the perfectly cooked fish below. Season the fish with salt and pepper and squeeze over some lemon juice before serving, with new potatoes and a green vegetable, such as griddled courgettes.

Slow-cooked cuttlefish stew

Cuttlefish can be grilled fast over fierce embers, but it also responds beautifully to slow cooking. Cuttlefish stew has become a bit of a River Cottage classic and it's one of my favourite ways to cook this wonderful ingredient. You'll need your fire to be really hot for searing the strips of cuttlefish before they go into the pot, but then the fire is allowed to die back and the dish is cooked gently over a medium heat.

Serves 6

1 cuttlefish (about 800g–1kg), cleaned, ink saved if possible
2 tbsp olive oil
250g bacon lardons
2 medium onions, peeled and thinly sliced
4 garlic cloves, peeled and thinly sliced
400g tin chopped tomatoes
2 tsp fennel seeds
Finely pared zest of 1 lemon
8 bay leaves
A good pinch of dried chilli flakes
About 1 litre fish, veg or chicken stock, or water
Sea salt and freshly ground black pepper

Prepare your fire (see pp.26–30).

Using a sharp knife, cut the cuttlefish body into 2–3cm strips and the tentacles into small pieces. Season with a little salt and pepper and trickle over 1 tbsp olive oil.

When the fire is really hot, set a close-meshed grill over it. It's ready when you can hover your hand above the grill for 1 second at most. Scatter the cuttlefish pieces across the grill, and cook for 4–5 minutes, until golden. Set aside on a plate.

Once the fire has died back a bit, set or hang a Dutch oven over it (you will need to construct a tripod of sorts to hang it) or put a heavy-based cast-iron pot on a grill over the fire. You want hot embers, but not so hot as to burn the food.

Add the remaining olive oil to the pot, then the bacon, and cook until golden and starting to caramelise. Add the onions and garlic and cook for 8–10 minutes until softened. Toss in the tomatoes, fennel seeds, lemon zest, bay leaves, chilli flakes and finally the browned cuttlefish and stir to combine. Add enough stock or water to just cover, then put a lid on the pot. Let it simmer for 1–2 hours, until the cuttlefish is very tender, topping up the liquid if it seems to be getting too low at any point.

When the cuttlefish is ready, take the pot off the heat and season the stew well with salt and pepper to taste. If you have the cuttlefish ink, stir it in at this point – it will darken and enrich the stew. Serve at once, with good bread and a crisp salad.

Mussels on fire

This is so simple, I would hardly even call it a recipe. Your fire must be going really well before you start because the mussels will give up some juice, which could dampen the spirit of an insubstantial fire. You will also need to use a close-mesh grill that won't let the mussels fall through into the fire. Once cooked, you can eat them straight from the shells – their briny flesh will be smoky and delicious.

You can use cultivated rope-grown muscles, or if you live near the coast you could collect your own. Found all around our coastline, wild mussels like exposed rocky shores with fast-flowing tides. The area between high and low water can be particularly plentiful, thanks to its seaweed and rock pools. Avoid collecting from May to August, as mussels will be underweight and prone to unsafe algal blooms, as well as higher levels of bacterial pollution. By October they will be plump and sweet. It's best to go for larger mussels, which will most likely have had a chance to breed already. Mussels high up on the rocks tend to be less gritty than those lower down, but they always benefit from soaking for several hours in salted water to purge them of any sand and grit. Once purged, scrub off any barnacles and pull off their 'beards'.

Serves 4 as a light snack
1kg fresh live mussels, cleaned

Get the fire going (see pp.26–30); it should be made up of really hot glowing coals (so that a little mussel juice won't extinguish them).

Rinse the mussels well and discard any that are open. If necessary, you can cook them in a couple of batches.

Place the grill over the fire and when it's really hot (you should be able to hover your hand above it for a maximum of 2 seconds), scatter over a single layer of mussels. As they begin to cook, which should be immediately, they will start to open and drip some of their juices. Use a pair of tongs to turn the mussels over, so they all get a good, even hit of heat.

After several minutes, the mussels will have opened up, indicating that they are cooked. Use the tongs to transfer the mussels to a bowl, discarding any that have failed to open.

The cooked mussels will be very hot so allow the shells to cool a little before you pick them up and take out the meat. Tuck in – these are delicious just as they are, perhaps with a few beers.

Scallops with garlic butter
and black pudding

Scallops come complete with their own little frying pans – their shells. If you can get hold of some live, hand-dived scallops in the shell this is a great thing to try on the fire. The sweet scallop meat takes on a superb flavour from the smoky embers, but it's the bubbling, garlicky butter with black pudding and a hint of rosemary that make this recipe so incredibly tasty.

Serves 2 as a starter

6–8 large scallops in their shells
100g butter, softened
100g black pudding, coarsely
    crumbled

2 garlic cloves, peeled and sliced
A couple of rosemary sprigs
Sea salt and freshly ground
    black pepper

Prepare your fire (see pp.26–30). You'll be cooking directly in the embers so they need to be super-hot.

It is possible to buy prepared scallops in the half-shell, ready to go, but if you're buying them live then you'll need to prepare them yourself. The shell will at first be shut tight, but it may well open up a few centimetres over 48 hours. To open or shuck the scallop you need a thin-bladed knife, such as a filleting knife – one with a little flex is good.

Hold the shell vertically (round-edge down on the board, hinge at the top) with the flat side of the shell facing towards you. Find an opening part-way down the edge of the shell to insert the knife into. If there is no opening, wangle the knife tip in anyway. The idea is to keep the knife as tight to the flat of the shell as you can, and carefully cut down through the muscle where it meets the shell.

With luck and practice, the shell will open and the scallop meat will remain whole. You need to get rid of the dark gut sac at the back of the scallop, plus a small strand of black intestine. Make a little incision just behind where the orange roe joins the meat and peel off the gubbins, leaving the orange roe with the meat (or you can remove the roe if you prefer). You may wish to cut off the small piece of extra-white tough muscle on the edge of the more tender flesh (as chefs often do); it's up to you.

Place each scallop nugget in its cleaned cupped half-shell and dot with the softened butter. Crumble over the black pudding and scatter over the sliced garlic. Season with plenty of salt and black pepper and add a little piece of rosemary sprig to each scallop shell.

Level out the glowing white embers of the fire with a stick, then carefully place the scallop shells directly onto the coals. The shells need to sit level. The scallops will heat up quickly and the butter will start to sizzle, frying the scallops in their own shells. After 1–2 minutes (depending on size), use tongs to turn each scallop over, without disturbing the shells.

Cook for a further minute, until the scallops are cooked through, then carefully remove each shell from the embers. If at any point you think the butter is burning, move the shell to a less-hot part of the fire.

Set the scallops on plates or stones and tuck in, but be careful of the hot shells. Serve with bread and a green salad.

Cockles cooked in seawater
with butter, garlic and parsley

This is a great one for the beach as, of course, that's the easiest place to find cockles. Low tide is the best time to delve into the sand. Simply plunge your fingers a few inches below the surface and feel for their hard corrugated shells.

The saltiness of the seawater you cook the cockles in is balanced by their natural sweetness and the garlic and butter. It is totally delicious. If you're cooking this at home, replace the seawater with ordinary tap water and add a splash of wine or cider.

Serves 2

A few large handfuls of cockles
100ml seawater, very lightly salted water, wine or cider

A large knob of unsalted butter
1 garlic clove, bashed
A handful of parsley, chopped

Prepare your fire. You want to be cooking over a good hot bed of embers and flaming logs (see pp.26–30).

Rinse the cockles well and discard any that are open.

When the fire is hot, set a grill over it; the temperature is right when you can hover your hand above the grill for a maximum of 2 seconds. Place a medium pan on the grill.

Put the seawater, butter and bashed garlic clove into the pan and put the lid on. When the water is boiling away, add the cockles and chopped parsley and give the pan a good shake. Replace the lid and cook, shaking once or twice, for 2–3 minutes or until the cockles are open.

Remove the pan from the heat and discard any cockles that have failed to open. Serve straight away, with good bread for dipping in the salty, buttery sauce.

Mushrooms with sage
and fried eggs

On a fine morning there's nothing nicer than cooking and eating breakfast outside. It turns a simple meal into something celebratory. In this recipe I'm using parasol mushrooms, a very tasty variety that grows wild around River Cottage in the early autumn, but you can use any large, open-cap mushroom. I love the flavour the mushrooms take on from the fire – it accentuates their earthy taste.

Serves 2

2 large open-cap mushrooms,
  such as parasols
2 tbsp olive oil
A large knob of butter

A small handful of sage leaves, chopped
2 eggs
Sea salt and freshly ground
  black pepper

Prepare your fire (see pp.26–30). When it is glowing nicely and the flames have died back, you're ready to cook.

Set a grill over the embers; you should be able to hover your hand above it for a maximum of 3 seconds.

Place the mushrooms, gill side down, on the grill and cook for 3–4 minutes. Turn them over, trickle over 1 tbsp olive oil and dot with most of the butter. Scatter over the chopped sage and season generously with salt and pepper. Cook for a further 5–8 minutes or until the mushrooms are looking soft and delicious.

Meanwhile, place a small, heavy frying pan on the grill. When it's hot, add the remaining 1 tbsp olive oil and the last of the butter. When it's bubbling away, crack in the eggs and cook for 2–3 minutes or until the whites are set and the yolks are cooked to your liking. Transfer to warmed plates, add the mushrooms and serve straight away.

Barbecued courgettes
with dill, goat's cheese, mint and yoghurt

Courgettes cook beautifully over fire. The high heat chars their surfaces and the smoke gives them a wonderful savoury depth. Here I'm pairing them with two of my favourite courgette accompaniments: goat's cheese and dill.

Serves 4 as a starter

4–6 medium courgettes
4 tbsp olive oil
Grated zest and juice of 1 lemon
½ tsp dried chilli flakes
2 tsp fennel seeds, toasted and crushed
3 tbsp natural yoghurt
150g soft goat's or ewe's cheese
½ small garlic clove, peeled and grated

A small bunch of chives, finely sliced
6–8 sprigs of dill, chopped, plus extra to garnish
2 tbsp chopped mint, plus whole leaves to garnish
Sea salt and freshly ground black pepper

Prepare your fire (see pp.26–30). You want a glowing bed of embers with no real flames to speak of.

Set a grill over the fire; it will have reached the right temperature when you can hover your hand above it for no more than 3 seconds.

Top and tail the courgettes and slice them lengthways into strips, 3–4mm thick. Place in a large bowl and season with salt and pepper. Add 2 tbsp olive oil along with the lemon zest, chilli flakes and fennel seeds, and tumble together.

Lay the courgettes across the grill. Cook for 8–12 minutes on each side, or until they are lightly and evenly charred, with some caramelisation.

Meanwhile, combine the remaining 2 tbsp olive oil with the yoghurt and crumble in the goat's cheese. Add the garlic and half of each of the herbs. Season with salt and pepper and mix well to combine.

Arrange the grilled courgettes over a large platter and squeeze over the lemon juice. Spoon on the goat's cheese dressing and scatter over the remaining herbs to serve.

Fried eggs and potatoes
with dried seaweed flakes

I once cooked this on the beach for breakfast; it was both simple and delicious. The fried eggs and potatoes are given a savoury quality by the addition of dried seaweed flakes, which are now easy to get hold of. If you can track down one of Mara's smoked seaweeds, then it'll taste even more amazing.

Serves 2

2 tbsp olive oil
200g cooked potatoes, sliced
1 tbsp dried seaweed flakes (smoked or unsmoked), such as dulse
25g butter

2 garlic cloves, peeled and thinly sliced
2 large free-range eggs
Sea salt and freshly ground black pepper

Get your fire going (see pp.26–30) and allow the flames to die back to hot embers.

Set a large frying pan over a hot area of the fire; it's at the right temperature when you can hover your hand above the frying pan for 2 seconds at most. Add the olive oil, followed by the potatoes. Cook them, tossing occasionally, for 8–12 minutes; they should begin to take on a little colour.

Add the seaweed flakes, along with the butter and garlic slices, and fry the potatoes for a further 5 minutes or so. Use a spatula to clear some space into which you can crack the eggs.

Carefully crack the eggs into the pan and continue to cook until they are done to your liking. Season everything with salt and pepper to taste, then serve.

Charred asparagus
with sheep's cheese and lemon thyme

Asparagus is one of the first vegetables of the year that really makes me want to head outdoors, light a fire and get cooking, and because it has a relatively short season I like to make the most of it when it's here. I think barbecuing is one of the best ways to cook this lovely slender veg: it takes on some smoky, charred notes that are wonderfully enhanced by the addition of sheep's cheese, olive oil and lemon thyme. You can keep the dish vegetarian – but it's also excellent served with good air-dried ham or salami.

Serves 2 as a starter

12–16 asparagus spears
A small bunch of lemon thyme
    (or ordinary thyme)
2 tbsp olive oil

100g hard sheep's cheese for grating,
    such as Berkswell or Pecorino
Sea salt and freshly ground
    black pepper

Prepare your fire (see pp.26–30). Once the flames die back and the embers are glowing very hot you'll be ready to cook.

Set a grill over the fire; it's at the right temperature when you can hover your hand above the grill for a maximum of 2 seconds. Snap the woody ends from the asparagus. Place the spears on a tray or in a large bowl. Strip the leaves from the thyme and scatter them over the asparagus, along with plenty of salt and pepper and the olive oil. Toss to coat.

Cook the asparagus on the grill for 3–4 minutes, turning occasionally. You want to encourage some charring and blistering. Transfer to a warm plate and grate over the cheese. Serve with air-dried ham or salami, if you like.

Grilled halloumi
with red onions and purple sprouting broccoli

This big, generous salad will satisfy everyone's hunger. There's nothing quite like the flavour of charred, bitter-sweet broccoli and the inclusion of sweet, caramelised onions and salty, tangy cheese brings the dish together beautifully. It's a real feast and illustrates how good vegetables can be when cooked over a fire. I like to serve a dish of simple harissa paste (p.132) on the side for dipping the veg into.

Serves 4

4–6 golf-ball-sized red onions, halved (skin on)

3–4 tbsp olive oil

300–400g purple sprouting broccoli, trimmed

250g block of halloumi cheese, cut into 1cm thick slices

A small bunch of thyme, leaves picked (optional)

1 tbsp red wine vinegar or cider vinegar

Sea salt and freshly ground black pepper

Prepare your fire (see pp.26–30). It needs to be moderately hot, with a large bed of glowing embers.

Set a grill over the fire; the temperature is right when you can hover your hand over it for a maximum of 4 seconds. Place the onion halves, cut side up, on the grill. Season with salt and pepper and trickle on a little olive oil. Cook for 15–20 minutes or until they are beginning to soften. Now turn them over and cook on their cut side for a further 15–20 minutes. Set the onions to one side; keep warm.

Place the trimmed broccoli in a large bowl, trickle with 2 tbsp olive oil and season with salt and pepper.

Stoke the fire and feed it if necessary – you want it fiercely hot now, so that you can hover your hand over the grill for 2 seconds at most. Arrange the broccoli over the grill and cook it for 4–5 minutes until beginning to soften and char around the edges. Move the broccoli to one side.

Lay the cheese on the grill and scatter over the thyme leaves, if using. Cook for a couple of minutes on each side or until golden and charring in places.

Transfer the hot broccoli to a warmed platter. Peel the charred skin from the onions and arrange the soft centres over the broccoli. Add the halloumi and give everything a final trickle of olive oil and vinegar. Serve with warm grilled sourdough.

Grilled cabbage
with caraway and garlic butter

Cabbage cooked in this way is just next level. Charring it a little – but not too much – lifts its natural sweetness while accentuating its slightly bitter flavour. Salty, bubbling garlic and caraway butter is an ideal accompaniment. Make sure you have a large-ish grill and a decent-sized fire so you have space to cook all the cabbage wedges at once.

Serves 4–6 as a starter or fireside snack

1 small cabbage, such as a Savoy or
   Hispi (Sweetheart)
100g salted butter
1 tbsp caraway seeds

1 small whole garlic bulb, cut in half
   around its 'equator'
Freshly ground black pepper

Prepare your fire (see pp.26–30). You want a good bed of hot embers, and the occasional flame won't hurt.

When the fire is hot, set a grill over it. Ideally there should be one area that is very hot where you can hover your hand above the grill for a maximum of 2 seconds, and another area that is less hot. You can achieve the less-hot area by raking back some of the hot embers – you should be able to hover your hand over the grill here for up to 4 seconds.

Cut the cabbage into 8–12 thin wedges, depending on size. Place these on the hotter part of the grill and cook for 2–4 minutes on each side; don't let them burn.

Meanwhile, heat a small pan on the less-hot part of the grill. Add the butter, caraway seeds and garlic bulb halves, cut side down. Season with plenty of black pepper. Allow the butter to melt and bubble way for 3–4 minutes.

When the cabbage wedges are softening in the middle and caramelising on the outside, lift them off the grill, dip into the garlicky caraway butter and eat at once.

Clay-baked onions

Clay-baked onions are sweet and utterly delicious. I love them served with nothing more than a trickle of olive oil and a little salt and pepper, but they also make a fabulous side to roast meat, fish or sausages.

Serves 4 as a side

A small bunch of sage
4 medium-large onions
Olive oil, for trickling
Flaky sea salt and freshly ground
    black pepper

You will also need
About 1kg natural potter's clay

Prepare your fire (see pp.26–30). It needs to be a combination of hot embers and flaming wood.

Divide the clay into 8 pieces, each about the size of a small apple. Form each piece into a disc, about 2.5cm thick.

Place one clay disc on a board, set a few sage leaves in the middle with some salt, and then place a whole, unpeeled onion on top. Trickle with olive oil and season with more salt and black pepper. Take a second clay disc and place it on top of the onion. Then gather up the edges of the clay to envelop the onion completely. Seal the seams well. Repeat this process for all the onions.

Nestle the clay spheres around the glowing embers of your fire, but not directly in them. Cook for about 1½ hours, turning the spheres every 15–20 minutes so they bake evenly. Take your time with this one: if the onions cook too fast, at too high a heat, the clay may crack and the onions could burn. You'll need to feed the fire during this time to maintain the heat.

Once the time is up, take the clay-wrapped onions out of the fire, using tongs or a tea towel. Use the back of a heavy cook's knife or simply a stone to crack the clay open, and carefully lift the onions out onto a board. It's worth doing just one first: it should be soft and tender inside.

Slice the onions in half and arrange them over a platter. Trickle with olive oil and sprinkle liberally with salt and pepper. Serve at once, with good bread, and perhaps some sausages.

Ember-baked autumn salad

Rather than use a grill for this recipe, I like to nestle the vegetables and fruit down in the hot embers of the fire instead. It's an incredibly simple way of cooking, but works a treat. There is no exact point at which the veg is 'perfectly done' since all these ingredients would be delicious raw anyway. It's down to personal preference. The outside of the celeriac and cabbage will take on some significant colour during their time in the fire, but that's the whole point – with that colour comes flavour. You simply slice away the charred skin and edges to reveal the steamed flesh inside.

Serves 8–12 as a side

2–3 small celeriac
1 small or medium red cabbage, cut
    in half or into quarters depending
    on size
4 medium red onions

4 eating apples
2–3 tbsp cider vinegar
2–3 tbsp extra virgin olive oil
Sea salt and freshly ground
    black pepper

Prepare a campfire (see pp.26–30); you want a large, regularly fed central fire that will produce lots of hot chunky embers.

Arrange the embers round the edge of the fire using a stick or some other tool, and place the vegetables (not the apples) directly onto them. Cook, turning frequently, until everything is tender in the middle – this may take up to 3 hours and even then the cabbage will probably still retain a little bite. Add the apples towards the end, as they will cook much more quickly. Don't worry if the vegetables burn on the outside – this is quite normal – but do watch the apples.

To check if the veg are soft enough to remove, lift them off the fire with some tongs and insert a small paring knife – it should meet with little, if any, resistance.

Peel the charred outer layer from the celeriac, cut the flesh into bite-sized pieces and place them in a warmed large serving bowl. Peel the charred outer layer from the cabbage, slice it thinly and add to the celeriac. Quarter and core the apples, slice into wedges and add these too.

Cut the soft onions in half and scoop out the sweet centres. Add these to the bowl, along with the cider vinegar, extra virgin olive oil and some salt and pepper. Tumble everything together well, then taste and adjust the seasoning.

Serve the salad as a side to some pork sausages, roast chicken or grilled venison. Alternatively, just crumble some goat's cheese over. Eat straight away.

Grilled beetroot
with labneh and dill

Cooking whole beetroot over a hot fire crisps and darkens the skins while sweetening and softening the flesh. I find it works best with new season beetroot, about golf ball size – just give them a quick scrub and chuck them on the grill, leaves and all. They only take 30–40 minutes to cook. Served with herbs, lemon and labneh (a simple homemade yoghurt cheese), they are delectable.

Serves 4 as a starter or a side

A large bunch of dill, chopped
About 3 tbsp olive oil
A good sprinkle of dried chilli flakes
Grated zest of 1 lemon
12 small, fresh beetroot, with the
    leafy tops if possible
Flaky sea salt and freshly ground
    black pepper

For the labneh
500ml natural cow's or sheep's
    yoghurt
½ tsp fine sea salt

First make the labneh. Put the yoghurt into a bowl, add the salt and give it a good mix. Line a sieve or colander with a large square of clean muslin or other fine cotton cloth. Spoon the salted yoghurt into the centre of the cloth, then gather up the sides. Tie the cloth at the top with kitchen string, enclosing the labneh in a bag.

Set the colander or sieve over a large bowl and leave the yoghurt to drain through for between 2 and 8 hours, depending on how thick you'd like the labneh.

Tip the drained labneh out of the cloth into a bowl. Add half the dill, 2 tbsp olive oil, the chilli flakes and half the lemon zest. Mix well and refrigerate until needed.

Prepare your fire (see pp.26–30). It should have a bed of smoky hot embers.

Set the grill in place; you'll know the temperature is right when you can hover your hand above it for 2 seconds at most. Arrange the beetroot on the grill and cook for 30–40 minutes or until tender when pierced with a knife, turning them regularly as they cook. The tops will smoke and burn, but this all adds to the theatre and the flavour. Don't worry if the beetroot blacken.

When the beetroot are cooked, thickly slice them and place in a dish with the labneh. Add plenty of salt and pepper, a little more olive oil and the remaining chopped dill, chilli flakes and lemon zest and tumble together. Bring to the table.

Blackened leeks
with hazelnuts and goat's cheese

At first, it might seem foolhardy to leave a few leeks in hot embers until they are black and charred, but cooked like this leeks are among the most delicious veg ever to rise out of the ashes. Under the charred outer skin you'll discover sweet, tender and incredibly moist flesh, which may need no more than a sprinkling of salt to bring it to life. Here I'm adding a light, soft goat's cheese, which goes beautifully with leeks, as well as some hazelnuts for added texture.

Serves 4

4 large leeks, washed (but untrimmed)
200g soft goat's cheese
A couple of handfuls of hazelnuts, lightly bashed

3–4 sprigs of thyme, leaves picked
4 tbsp extra virgin olive oil
Sea salt and freshly ground black pepper

Prepare your fire (see pp.26–30). It needs to be really hot to cook the leeks properly, so make sure you have a nice bed of hot embers before you start cooking.

Place the leeks straight on the hot embers, or lay them on a grill that's as close to the fire as you can get it. Cook the leeks until they are deeply charred on the outside and feel soft in the middle. This can take anywhere between 10 and 20 minutes, depending on the heat. You'll have to turn and rotate the leeks at intervals to ensure they cook evenly.

Once they are ready (completely blackened), transfer the leeks to a board and cut them in half from top to bottom. Lift the tender centres away from the charred outer layer and lay on four serving plates. Season them well with salt and pepper.

Crumble over the goat's cheese and scatter on the hazelnuts. 'Bruise' the thyme leaves by scrunching them with your fingers, then scatter them over the cheese. Finish each leek with a good trickle of extra virgin olive oil, then serve.

Wood-roast sprout salad
with apple and celeriac

I know a barbecue is the last thing you tend to think of when sprouts are in the offing. But although it may be cold outside, this is a great winter warmer. You don't have to spend hours shivering outdoors either – simply get your fire going and when it's ready to cook over, nip out and scatter the sprouts over the grill. Give them a tumble every so often, then hoik them off and you're done. You can now disappear indoors and throw the salad together.

Serves 4

500g firm Brussels sprouts
2 tbsp olive oil
250g celeriac
2 crunchy eating apples
Juice of ½ lemon
Sea salt and freshly ground
    black pepper

For the dressing
2 tsp caster sugar
2 tsp English or Dijon mustard
1 tbsp cider vinegar
2 tbsp extra virgin olive oil
2 tbsp natural yoghurt
A bunch of tarragon, finely chopped,
    plus extra leaves to serve

Trim the Brussels sprouts by cutting the very base off each sprout then peel away any tired outer leaves. Place the sprouts in a bowl and trickle on the olive oil, then season well with salt and pepper and tumble together.

Prepare your fire (see pp.26–30) and when the flames have died back and you have a good even bed of hot embers, set a grill in place. The temperature is right when you can hover your hand above the grill for no more than 2 seconds.

Carefully scatter the seasoned sprouts over the grill. Cook, turning regularly, for 8–10 minutes or until charred on the outside and soft in the middle. Lift the sprouts off the grill and return them to the bowl, then head back to the kitchen.

To make the dressing, combine all the ingredients in a bowl and stir well, seasoning with salt and pepper to taste.

Peel and thinly slice the celeriac, then cut into thin matchsticks. Quarter, core and thinly slice the apples. Toss the celeriac and apples in the lemon juice and then add to the sprouts. Trickle over half the dressing and tumble everything together.

Pile the salad onto a serving platter, spoon over the remaining dressing and finish with a scattering of tarragon leaves.

Grilled Jerusalem artichokes
with tahini yoghurt

I like the way gnarled, knobbly Jerusalem artichokes cook over the heat of a fire, because thanks to their shape and irregular size, there will always be some areas of the vegetable that are more cooked than others. You can actually eat Jerusalem artichokes completely raw so, for me, any point between that and meltingly soft works! Tahini, a paste made from sesame seeds, is the main player in the rather delicious dressing I use for this warm salad. Tahini has a real affinity with the earthy, woody-tasting Jerusalem artichokes.

Serves 4

1kg Jerusalem artichokes, scrubbed
Olive oil, to drizzle
A handful of 'hard' herbs, such as
    rosemary, sage and thyme
100ml natural yoghurt
50g light tahini

½ garlic clove, peeled and grated
Juice of ½ lemon
2 handfuls of mixed salad leaves
Sea salt and freshly ground
    black pepper

Prepare your fire (see pp.26–30). You want a moderately hot bed of glowing embers.

Set a large grill over the fire; it's at the right temperature when you can hover your hand above it for no more than 3 seconds.

Drizzle the Jerusalem artichokes with a little olive oil then place them on the grill. Sprinkle over a little sea salt and the herbs. Cook for about 35–40 minutes, turning the artichokes regularly. It's nice to have a mixture of small, tender artichokes and big crunchy ones.

Meanwhile, put the yoghurt into a small bowl and stir in the tahini. Add a drizzle of olive oil, the garlic and the lemon juice. Mix together and season with salt and pepper to taste.

Once the Jerusalem artichokes are cooked to your liking, slice them thickly. Lay the salad leaves out over a big sharing platter. Add the artichokes and drizzle over the tahini yoghurt dressing. Finish with a final drizzle of olive oil, a squeeze of lemon and some more black pepper and sea salt if you feel the artichokes need it.

A simple harissa paste

Traditionally used in North African cuisine, harissa is a vibrant, spicy paste, full of chilli, garlic, coriander and cumin. This is a great little recipe to have in your repertoire, and something to have jarred up and ready to go at any time, as it makes a fantastic accompaniment to all sorts of grilled and roasted food. You can roast the chillies directly in the embers, as I do here, or cook them on a grill set over the embers.

Makes a 400g jar

4–6 large red chillies
1 tsp coriander seeds
½ tsp cumin seeds
4 garlic cloves, peeled and sliced
½ tsp flaky sea salt

A squeeze of lemon juice
2 tsp tomato purée
1 tbsp olive oil, plus extra to store
   the harissa

Prepare your fire (see pp.26–30). You want a hot bed of glowing embers.

Carefully lay the chillies directly on top of the hot embers and let them cook, turning often, until the skins blacken and the flesh is tender. Place the cooked chillies in a bowl, then cover and allow to cool completely.

Remove the stalks from the cooled chillies and peel off the skins. Split the chillies open, then scrape out the seeds with a knife and discard them.

Toast the coriander and cumin seeds in a dry frying pan for a few minutes until fragrant, making sure they don't burn. Tip the toasted seeds into a mortar and bash them up well with the pestle.

Add the chillies, garlic and salt to the mortar and continue to bash until you have a juicy paste. Finally stir in the lemon juice, tomato purée and olive oil.

Either serve the harissa straight away or transfer it to an airtight container, cover the surface with a film of olive oil and store in the fridge until needed; it will keep for 2 weeks.

Campfire bread

Baking bread in a pot in the fire is an absolute joy. The secret to success is to create an even heat around the bread while it bakes, and to prevent it scorching on the base. Build your fire with a hardwood such as oak or beech, which will give a consistent heat. Choose a decent, heavy cast-iron pot with a lid – a small Dutch oven is ideal, or a casserole you're happy to place in the fire. I put the bottom of an old springform cake tin into the base of the pot too, on top of a few small pebbles. This creates a gap between pot and bread, which helps prevent scorching.

Makes 1 loaf

250g strong white bread flour, plus extra for dusting
250g wholemeal or malted bread flour

5g fast-action dried yeast
10g fine sea salt
300ml warm water
A little sunflower oil

Mix the flours, yeast and salt together in a large bowl. Add the water and mix, using one hand, to a soft, sticky, easily kneadable dough, adding a little more flour or water if necessary. Turn out onto a lightly floured surface. Wipe out the bowl. Knead the dough until it's smooth, stretchy and no longer sticky, about 10 minutes. Shape into a rough round and rub the surface with a little oil. Put the dough into the clean bowl and cover the bowl with cling film. Leave to rise in a warm place until doubled in size, which should take about an hour or so.

Turn the risen dough out onto your surface – this will knock a lot of the air out of it. Gently stretch the top and bottom edges and fold them into the middle. Repeat with the left and right edges. With each fold, crimp the seam of the edges together. Turn the dough over and use your hands to form it into a nice, tight round shape.

Place the dough, smooth side down, in a floured proving basket or bowl lined with a floured clean tea towel. Cover it loosely with a tea towel and leave to prove in a warm place for 20–30 minutes. This is now the time to get your fire going (see pp.26–30). You want a mixture of burning wood and chunky glowing embers.

Take a heavy-based cast-iron pot, spread a few small pebbles over the bottom and lay the base of a springform cake tin on top; it should be a snug fit. Cut out a round of baking parchment, using the cake-tin base as a template; set it aside for later.

When your fire is ready, clear an area within it, so that the pot will be able to sit directly on the earth rather than on the embers. This ensures that most of the heat will reach the loaf from the sides and the top of the pot, and not from underneath.

Put the lid on the pot and transfer it to the cleared area to heat up. When the dough is ready and the pot is hot, lift the lid. Lay the baking parchment in the base of the pot. Carefully ease the dough straight into the pot. Put the lid on and use your tongs to arrange some large embers around and on top of the pot.

Bake for up to 1 hour, until cooked through, keeping the heat as consistent as possible by shuffling embers about, feeding the fire and rotating the pot every 10–15 minutes. Don't be afraid to lift the lid and check on the bread's progress during cooking – it's the only sure way to get the best results. To test the loaf, take it out and tap it on its underside; it should sound hollow. When baked, carefully tip the loaf out of the hot pot and let it cool, at least partially, on a wire rack before slicing. If it's overly blackened in any one area, just cut this off.

Simple flatbreads

Quick to make, tear-and-share flatbreads are perfect for cooking over an open fire. I have a cast-iron frying pan that I keep especially for this purpose. It's a robust old thing, which I sit directly in the embers. When it's smoking hot I lay the flatbreads down in the pan and they cook very quickly. You could use a large flat stone instead – just make sure it's really hot.

Makes 8

250g plain flour, plus extra for dusting
1 tsp fine sea salt
150ml warm water

4 tbsp extra virgin olive or rapeseed oil, plus extra to serve
Flaky sea salt, to finish

Sift the flour into a large bowl and add the salt. Measure the water in a jug, stir in the oil and pour this into the flour in a thin stream, stirring well with a wooden spoon or your hands to form a slightly sticky dough.

Turn the dough out onto a lightly floured surface and knead for about 5 minutes, until it feels smooth and plump, sprinkling on a little more flour only if the dough feels very sticky. Let the dough rest while you light the fire.

Prepare your fire (see pp.26–30). It wants to be hot for this recipe: you need a good bed of glowing embers, and a little flame is fine.

When you're ready to cook and eat the flatbreads, roll the dough into a sausage shape and divide it into 8 pieces. Roll each piece into a ball. Flour your work surface or board and a rolling pin, then roll out each ball into a circle, 2–3mm thick, using plenty of flour as the dough is liable to stick.

Set a heavy-based cast-iron frying pan over the fire and wait until it's very hot; you should be able to hover your hand above it for a maximum of 2 seconds.

Shake off any excess flour from one of the flatbreads and lay it in the hot pan. Let it sit for a minute or two, until the dough looks 'set' on top and is starting to lift away from the pan. Carefully look at the underside and, if you can see dark brown patches forming, flip the flatbread over and cook the other side for 30–45 seconds. If the flatbread appears to be colouring too quickly, move the pan to a cooler part of the fire.

Wrap the cooked flatbread in a cloth while you cook the others. To serve the flatbreads, trickle with extra virgin oil, then sprinkle over a pinch of flaky salt.

Potato stickbreads
with seaweed

I've enriched this dough with dried seaweed flakes and mashed potato, two simple ingredients that give it an umami-like quality. You could use the dough to make flatbreads and cook them in a cast-iron pan (as for the previous recipe), but I prefer to twirl it around some freshly cut sticks and toast it over the fire – it's just sheer pleasure. Thin lengths of green hazel work well but any clean, straight stick will suffice.

You can make the dough the day before you intend to use it – leave it in the fridge during the proving stage and take it out a few hours before you need it.

Makes 6 sticks

2 medium baking potatoes
400g strong white bread flour,
    plus extra for dusting
1 tsp fine sea salt
2 tsp fast-action dried yeast
2 tbsp dried seaweed flakes
Up to 250ml water
A few hard herbs, such as sprigs
    of rosemary or thyme, or some
    bay leaves (optional)

You will also need

6 sticks, at least 1cm in diameter
    and 40cm long

First bake your potatoes: preheat an oven to 200°C/Gas mark 6, prick the potatoes all over with a fork and bake them in the oven for about 1 hour 20 minutes or until they are completely tender right through when you poke a small knife into the middle of them.

When cool enough to handle, halve the potatoes and scoop out the soft potato flesh into a bowl. Mash until smooth and set aside to cool.

Place the flour, salt, yeast and dried seaweed flakes into a large bowl. Add enough water to make a soft, sticky dough, then transfer the dough to a lightly floured surface and knead for 5 minutes until it begins to feel soft and smooth.

Stretch out the dough on a floured surface and spread the mashed potato evenly on top of it. Knead for another couple of minutes to combine the potato thoroughly with the dough. Shape the dough into a rough round (pic 1 overleaf) and transfer it to a large bowl.

Cover the bowl with cling film and leave the dough to rise at room temperature for 1½–2 hours.

Turn the dough out onto a lightly floured surface. Divide it into 6 equal balls and roll each one back and forth to make a 20–30cm long, thin cylinder (pic 2); use a little more flour if necessary to prevent the dough sticking. Let the dough lengths sit for 10 minutes.

Now you can start twirling the dough. Pinch one end of a length of dough against a stick so it adheres. Now turn the dough round the stick so it spirals all the way to the tip, embedding a small sprig of rosemary or thyme or some bay leaves in the dough as you turn it (pic 3), if you like. Pinch the end to fix it in place. Make sure you leave yourself a 'handle' at one end with no dough on it. Repeat with the rest of the dough.

Hold the dough-wrapped sticks over the hot embers (pic 4), turning often to ensure even cooking and minimal charring (though a little charring is rather nice), until the dough has increased in size and is golden brown and crisp all over. This should take 15–20 minutes.

Leave the bread until cool enough to handle, then tear it into pieces to eat. You can dip it in olive oil and scatter it with salt, if you like, or smear it with salty butter.

Baked peaches
with vanilla, butter, thyme and brown sugar

This wonderful late-summer dessert is easy to assemble and incredibly delicious. It's the perfect thing to cook as the flames die back and you are left with a nice bed of chunky embers. You can do the same thing with apples or plums; they will be equally good.

Serves 4

4 ripe peaches
50g unsalted butter, softened
1 vanilla pod, split lengthways

2 tbsp soft brown sugar
Grated zest of ½ lemon
4 sprigs of thyme

Prepare your fire (see pp.26–30) and let it die back a bit. You want a nice bed of moderately hot embers – a little flaming wood and smoke is fine.

Halve the peaches and remove the stone. Lay the peach halves, cut side up, on a double layer of foil, large enough to encase the peaches in a parcel.

Put the butter into a bowl. Scrape the vanilla seeds from the pod and add them to the butter, along with the sugar and lemon zest; mix well. Dot a little of this sweet vanilla butter on each peach half. Top with the sprigs of thyme and throw in the split vanilla pod for good measure. Fold the foil over the peaches to create a neat sealed parcel.

Set the parcel carefully down in the embers of the fire. The peaches need to be cooked in a gentle, glowing heat, so don't let them come into contact with any super-hot embers. Bake for 20–25 minutes, rotating the parcel occasionally to ensure the peaches cook evenly.

Remove the parcel, open it and check if the fruit is tender by prodding it with a knife. If it's not quite ready, rewrap and return to the fire for a little longer. Once the peaches are tender, serve them hot, with all the buttery sweet juices from the parcel, and cream if you like.

Grilled pears in honey
and cinnamon with vanilla mascarpone

I was first cooked this by River Cottage chef Conner Reed. It was absolutely delicious – so much so that it's now become a firm favourite of mine. If the pears are ripe they won't take long to cook so the fire can be a little hotter; if they are on the firm side, take things a bit slower, giving the fruit time to tenderise.

Serves 2

2 medium-large pears
2 tbsp honey
1 vanilla pod, split lengthways,
    seeds removed and reserved

½ cinnamon stick
200g mascarpone
1 tbsp icing sugar
50g flaked almonds, toasted

Prepare your fire (see pp.26–30). You want a bed of moderately hot embers with no real flames.

Set a grill over the fire; it will have reached the right temperature when you can hover your hand above it for no more than 3 seconds.

To prepare the pears, cut each one into 6 equal wedges and remove the core. Place flesh side down on the hot grill and colour lightly on all sides. Meanwhile, put the honey, empty vanilla pod and cinnamon stick in a cast-iron pan on the grill and warm gently.

Once the pears are brown, add them to the pan and let them soften gently in the bubbling honey; this should take around 5 minutes.

In the meantime, in a bowl, mix the mascarpone with the vanilla seeds and icing sugar to combine.

Once the pears are soft, place spoonfuls of the mascarpone in the pan, along with the toasted almonds, and allow the mascarpone to melt slightly. Serve immediately.

Cider and fennel toffee apple

This recipe was given to me by River Cottage chef Mark Mecabe and it is, without doubt, the best version of a toffee apple I've ever had. The fennel seeds and cider work so well with the crunchy, salty, smoky caramel. On bonfire night, especially, it's such fun for everyone to dip their own apple in the caramel.

Makes 8–10

8–10 firm eating apples
500g caster sugar
500ml medium-dry cider

2 tbsp fennel seeds,
	coarsely crushed
A pinch of flaky sea salt

Bring a pan of water to the boil, take it off the heat and add the apples. Let them steep for a minute or so, to remove the waxy coating on the skin (this will enable the caramel to stick better).

Dry the apples thoroughly and skewer each one with a sturdy stick, capable of holding its weight.

Prepare your fire (see pp.26–30). You want a bed of moderately hot embers with no real flames.

Set a grill over the fire; it will have reached the right temperature when you can hover your hand above it for no more than 3 seconds.

Put the sugar and cider into a heavy cast-iron pan and place on the grill over the hot fire. Bring to a simmer, then cook steadily, without stirring, to form a golden brown caramel (roughly the colour of autumn leaves); this will take 10–15 minutes. It's important to keep an eye on it to make sure it doesn't boil over or darken too much. The caramel needs to reach the 'hard crack stage', when it will register 150°C on a cook's thermometer. (Or you can test it by dropping a little into cold water– it should harden instantly; if it's soft and squidgy, cook it for a few minutes longer.)

When the caramel has reached the correct stage, remove the pan from the heat and vigorously stir in the fennel seeds and sea salt.

To coat each apple, hold by the stick and carefully dip it into the hot caramel, then turn the apple in the caramel until well coated and glistening. Allow the caramel coating to cool and set before eating.

The Earth Oven

With the exception of miners, geologists and grave-

diggers, human beings tend to stay very much on the surface of the earth and I imagine few people, in the Western world at least, will have ever dug a hole in the ground in which to cook their supper. Hopefully this chapter will change that, with a technique that relies on the basic principle of creating heat in a dug-out pit, and trapping it there by re-covering it with soil.

Cooking in the earth is a technique that has been practised in different ways and by different cultures for many thousands of years. The most famous earth ovens – or pit ovens, as they're also known – are those of the Māori people of New Zealand. These were in use from the time of the first Māori settlements in the country, probably about 700 years ago, and evolved from an even older Polynesian tradition. Earth ovens, called hāngi, remain a part of Māori culture today; they are a simple and effective way to cook both large and smaller quantities of food.

There are different ways of constructing a hāngi, but at its most basic, a large hole is dug in the ground and a fire is set either in its base or next to it. Stones are placed in the fire and when they are as hot as they'll get (which is very hot) they are arranged in the base of the hole. Raw food is placed on the stones and covered with a layer of leaves or cloth, and then everything is buried under a layer of earth. The earth retains the heat incredibly well and the food cooks gently, sometimes for many hours.

In essence, a hāngi is just like a modern domestic oven – cooking food with a heat source contained inside an insulated space.

Making a hāngi

When I make an earth oven at home or at River Cottage, I do it in the style of a traditional hāngi. The dimensions of the hole and the size of the stones will depend on what I intend to cook. But given the effort involved in preparing the pit and the fire, I usually cook quite a lot of food for a fair-sized group and I'd recommend you do the same. Besides, this is such an unusual and fascinating way to cook that it should definitely be shared with friends and family.

Weekends are perfect for making an earth oven. You can plan ahead and think about what you would like to cook and who you might like to invite to share the feast. You'll have time to dust off the spade and find a good patch of ground to make the pit.

The end goal of this gastronomic undertaking is, of course, the 'big reveal' when you uncover and lift the delicious food from the earth. Think Christmas, but muddier – it really is like unwrapping a present: the suspense, the trepidation, the relief, the occasional disappointment (easy fix), and the joy. These are emotions we

experience with other forms of cooking, but they are heightened here because you simply do not know what's going on deep down there below the hot steamy clods, and there's no way to really check.

You can insert a digital probe thermometer into the food before you bury it, with a wire that leads above ground, to tell you exactly when it's done – but I'm not convinced the Māori would approve. It would be like saying you're going to navigate the oceans by the stars, but then taking your GPS along.

Digging the pit

Choose a sensible location for your hāngi: it should be sited on level ground, with plenty of clear space around it for you to set a fire in which to heat the cooking stones. The fire needs to be substantial and to burn steadily for up to 2½ hours to get the stones hot, so don't dig your hāngi too close to buildings, trees, fences or any structure that could catch fire.

Think about the soil too: if it's solid clay or full of rocks, or if the ground has been hardened lately by drought, digging will be a very tough task. Try to find somewhere with reasonably soft, easy-digging soil.

There is nothing complex about the hole itself. It is simply a cavity deep enough to fit both stones and food in, covered with a good layer of earth. A basic garden spade is the best tool for the job. If you're siting your hāngi in a grassy area, remove the turf in fairly neat patches before digging. Put these aside, to be replaced later.

The depth of the hole will, of course, dictate how much earth you can then put back over the food, to keep the heat in. I've found a foot (30cm) or so of earth to be adequate. I usually make the hole square or rectangular, but you could make a circular hole (or any shape, for that matter).

A hāngi can be used more than once. Once I have dug one, it tends to get several uses, particularly during the warmer months. In between times, I make sure the hole itself is covered with thick branches or planks, so that no one steps into it. The pile of earth at the side of the pit I just leave as it is – perhaps covering it with a tarpaulin if it's likely to be standing unused for more than a few weeks, to discourage the growth of grass or other plants, and so that it doesn't erode.

The sides of a hāngi can start to crumble a bit, so before each use I tidy the hole with a spade, scraping out any loose earth or ash or remnants from the last cook-up. This, along with a bit of unavoidable wastage every time you shovel soil in and out of a hāngi, means you lose a little bit of soil volume over time. Over the course of a few uses, you might need to replenish the soil with a shovel or two more from another location.

After around 4 months I'd suggest filling in the hole, re-covering it with turf, and digging a fresh hole next time you fancy a cook-up. There's no reason not to dig it again in the same place.

Stones and bricks

You never really know whether a stone will crack in the heat of the fire – it depends on where it came from and how much moisture it has in it. As a rule, metamorphic rocks (those that have been exposed to varying degrees of heat and pressure), including quartzite, slate, granulite and schist, should be safe to use for your hāngi, as well as igneous rocks, formed through the cooling and solidification of magma or lava, such as basalt, diorite and gabbro. The stones you use should be large-ish – nothing smaller than a grapefruit – but of course not so big that you can't lift them! Don't worry too much about shape, although relatively flat stones heat more quickly and are a bit easier to arrange in the base of the hāngi.

If such rocks and stones elude you, you can use 'fire bricks' instead. Also called refractory bricks, these are the type of bricks used to line kilns, furnaces, fireboxes and hearths and they are designed to withstand and retain large amounts of heat, which is exactly what you want. They look like house bricks, only lighter in colour. They are slightly heftier in price too but once you have them they'll last you a long time and they come in useful for other outdoor cooking – such as the Fire-bricked steaks on p.66.

When it comes to judging how many stones to use, my rule of thumb is: roughly a third of the volume of the food you are cooking. The amount of stone dictates the level of heat so I might use fewer stones with very tender ingredients that need less heat, such as fish, or more stones with tougher pieces of meat.

The fire

It is essential that the stones or bricks of the hāngi are super-charged with heat before you start cooking. Some hāngi cooks like to set a fire for heating the stones in the base of the pit itself, so that the stones will be in situ from the outset. However, I prefer to build the fire on the ground beside the pit. This means that once the stones are hot, I can roll or lift half of them into the pit, arranging them on the base, then add the food, before placing the remainder of the stones around and over it. I like to keep the adjacent fire going during the course of cooking too. It's handy for grilling other elements of the meal, or to finish off cooking food from the hāngi if necessary.

Begin by building a large fire, following the technique on pp.26–30. When the fire is blazing well, arrange your stones/bricks in and around it, then add more firewood to effectively envelop the stones. As that enveloping wood burns, it will heat the stones or bricks. To keep the heat travelling into them, you must continue to feed the fire. As the wood burns and turns to embers, the stones will naturally shift and move. Have a hefty pair of metal tongs to hand so you can rearrange the stones or bricks as necessary, keeping them in the heart of the fire. It will take at least 1½ hours for them to get sufficiently hot for the hāngi.

If you're using bricks, you'll see them glowing in places when they are ready. You won't necessarily see this change of colour with natural stones, so time is the best indication of when they're ready. The only way to actually measure the precise heat of the stones or bricks is to use a point-and-shoot thermometer: you want the stones to be at least 400°C before they go into the hāngi pit.

Burying the meat, vegetables or fish

Make sure you have your food ready to go before you put the first batch of stones in position. You will also need a large piece of hessian or another coarse fabric, soaked in water and wrung out, to cover the food.

Begin by using the heavy-duty tongs or a spade to transfer about half the stones from the fire to the pit, forming a layer that roughly covers the base of the pit. Next, to separate the food slightly from the intense heat of the stones, lay down a few thin sticks or pieces of hardwood kindling. Alternatively, a few handfuls of damp seaweed work well. You could also use cuttings of 'hard' herbs such as rosemary, bay, juniper, thyme or sage to give your food an intense aromatic flavour as it steams and bakes over the hot rocks.

Place your chosen ingredients (leg of lamb, vegetables, shellfish) on top of this dividing layer, then cover with more of the same material (seaweed, herbs etc.) or something different, perhaps. Arrange the rest of the hot stones around and on top of the food.

To keep the soil out of direct contact with the food, take the piece of wet hessian or other fabric, fold it several times to make a thick layer, then drape it over the stones. Carefully tuck the hessian down around the stones and food as neatly as possible, then gradually pile the earth you have dug out of the pit back into it. Put any turf or clumps of earth bound by vegetation back in place on top – this denser, more matted layer helps to seal the heat and steam in, and looks nice and neat at the same time.

Cooking time

Earth oven cooking times are quite tricky to give with precision but are generally pretty similar to those of the baking temperature in a domestic oven, so base your 'below ground timings' on that starting point. I'd also suggest that half the fun is in 'not knowing'. The worst thing that can happen is your food emerges overcooked. You can't do an awful lot about that, but it's hardly the end of the world. If your food comes out undercooked, on the other hand, it's easily fixed. You can just finish the cooking over your adjacent wood fire or in your kitchen oven.

When you're ready to take the food out of the ground, do so with great care because it's really important to keep the gritty earth away from the food. Think of yourself as a gastronomic archaeologist unearthing a precious find. Don't just go at it with the spade, as you'll disturb everything beneath. Use a small trowel or your hands to carefully lift the earth away. When you get down to the damp hessian, gather up the edges and fold them inwards to envelop any crumbs of loose earth, then lift it cleanly out of the pit or fold it neatly out of the way. Now you can use your tongs to lift away the stones (which will still be hot) and whatever else you used to cover the food.

Unless the weather is really dire, I think you should definitely eat your earth oven meal outdoors. It will ensure that the event feels like a real celebration.

Autumn vegetable pit bake

This pit bake is all about the veg. It will take time to cook, but it's worth the wait. Once revealed, the juices and the fragrant herby notes make for a rather incredible autumn feast, bursting with sweetness and smoky, earthy character.

Leave all the vegetables whole and unpeeled – just give them a scrub before you bury them. They are going back into the soil they came from, after all.

Serves 10–12

4–6 small branches of bay
   (with lots of leaves)
A large bunch of sage
A large bunch of rosemary
6 medium red onions
3–6 assorted squash, about
   2kg in total
6 medium beetroot
6 whole garlic bulbs
6 potatoes, about 2kg
6 fennel bulbs
2 tbsp cider vinegar

8 tbsp olive oil
A large bunch of flat-leaf parsley,
   leaves picked and chopped
Sea salt and freshly ground
   black pepper
Hard goat's or ewe's cheese,
   to serve (optional)

You will also need
10 fire bricks or equivalent large stones
A large square of hessian

Light a large fire next to the spot where you intend to dig your pit. Put your fire bricks or stones into the fire to heat up (see p.155). It will take between 1½ and 2½ hours of consistent heating before they are ready, so you'll need to keep feeding the fire.

Meanwhile, dig a tidy hole with clean sides and a flat base, about 60cm square and 40–50cm deep (see p.152). Soak a large piece of hessian, roughly 2 metres square, in a bucket of fresh water for a few minutes.

Using heavy-duty tongs or a spade, arrange half the hot stones or bricks over the base of the pit then scatter over some thin sticks. Lay half of the bay branches over the sticks, add half the sage and rosemary, then arrange all the vegetables in an even layer over the herbs. Scatter over the remaining sage and rosemary and place more bay on top. Arrange the remaining stones over and around everything.

Lift the hessian out of the bucket, wring out the water and fold it in half, then in half again. Carefully lay the wet hessian down over the vegetables, tucking it in around the edges. It'll be very steamy and smoky.

Gradually back-fill the soil and pack down any clumps of turf neatly over the top. Allow the veg to cook for about 2 hours.

After this time, carefully lift the turf and earth away. Try to get as much of it out as possible, so you are left with a relatively soil-free piece of hessian in place. Gather this up as carefully as you can and lift it out of the pit, avoiding any soil falling down onto the vegetables.

Remove the twigs and herbs and use your tongs to lift the veg out onto a large board. Halve all the veg and season with lots of flaky salt and pepper. Combine the cider vinegar and olive oil and trickle generously over everything. Scatter over the chopped parsley. Lastly, and optionally, a good grating of hard goat's/ewe's cheese is very hard to beat.

Pit-baked leg of lamb

Lamb has an earthy, almost herbaceous flavour that is accentuated by the natural flavours you get from cooking below ground. In this recipe, a leg of lamb is laid on a smouldering bed of rosemary and fennel tops, then draped with large chard leaves to protect it from the soil. You could also try a shoulder of wild venison, an organic or free-range chicken, or a rolled shoulder of rare-breed pork.

The earth oven essentially steam-cooks food, so it doesn't create the dark, caramelised flavour notes you get with roasting. With this in mind, I sometimes like to brown the meat over the fire before I put it in the pit. This gives the best of both worlds, and also kick-starts the cooking process.

Serves 6

A whole leg of lamb or hogget,
   about 2kg
2 tbsp olive oil
A few handfuls of rosemary stems
   and fennel tops or other woody
   herbs, such as thyme
A few handfuls of large chard or
   spinach leaves
Sea salt and freshly ground
   black pepper
Salsa verde (p.77), to serve

You will also need
6 fire bricks or equivalent large stones
A large square of hessian

Take the lamb out of the fridge several hours before you intend to cook it and allow it to come up to room temperature.

Light a large fire next to the spot where you intend to dig your pit. Put your fire bricks or stones into the fire to heat up (see p.155). It will take between 1½ and 2½ hours of consistent heating before they are ready, so you'll need to keep feeding the fire.

Meanwhile, dig a tidy hole with clean sides and a flat base, about 60–70cm long, 40–50cm wide and 50cm deep (see p.152). Soak a large piece of hessian, roughly 2 metres square, in a bucket of fresh water for a few minutes.

Rub the meat all over with olive oil and season it well with salt and black pepper. Then place it on a grill set over the fire for 4–5 minutes on each side, until it's taken on a golden, caramelised colour.

Use your heavy-duty tongs or a spade to lift half the hot stones out of the fire and place them in the base of the pit.

Lay a few thin sticks over the stones, then create a bed of your chosen herbs on top and place the lamb in position. Working quickly, cover with more herbs and drape the chard or spinach leaves over the lamb. Arrange the remaining stones around and over the joint.

Wring out the hessian and fold it over a couple of times, then carefully lay it over the stones, tucking it in neatly around the edges. Everything will be steamy and smoky, but don't worry about that.

Gently fill the hole, scattering earth over the hessian. Once the earth is level with the ground, rearrange the sods of turf you initially removed over the surface and press them into place. Leave the meat to cook for about 3 hours.

Carefully lift off the turf and dig the earth away – try to get as much of it out as possible, so you are left with a relatively soil-free piece of hessian in place. Gather this up as carefully as you can and lift it out of the pit, avoiding any soil falling down onto the lamb below.

Remove the herbs and use the tongs to lift the meat out onto a large board. Leave the lamb to rest for 20 minutes before carving. Serve with salsa verde, new potatoes and a dressed tomato salad.

Pit-baked lobsters
in seaweed with aïoli

This is a great way to cook whole lobsters. They steam gently and evenly in the seaweed and stay lovely and moist. In addition, their hard shells mean you can rinse off any stray earth after they are cooked. I sometimes do this on a beach – I simply freeze and kill the lobsters at home, then transport them to my cook-site. You could also try this approach with crabs, large fish, mussels or clams.

Serves 2

2 live lobsters, 1–1.5kg each
A bucket of fresh, damp seaweed,
    such as kelp or bladderwrack
Sea salt and freshly ground
    black pepper

For the aïoli
2 very fresh egg yolks
2 garlic cloves, peeled and grated,
    then crushed to a paste
1 heaped tsp Dijon mustard
1 tbsp cider vinegar or lemon juice
200ml light olive oil
200ml sunflower oil

To serve
Lemon wedges

You will also need
4 fire bricks or equivalent large stones

Light a large fire next to the spot where you intend to dig your pit. Put your fire bricks or stones into the fire to heat up (see p.155). It will take between 1½ and 2½ hours of consistent heating before they are ready, so you'll need to keep feeding the fire.

In the meantime, dig your pit, with clean sides and a flat base, approximately 40–50cm square and 30–40cm deep (see p.152). Place the live lobsters in a freezer for 45 minutes, to sedate them.

To make the aïoli, whisk the egg yolks, garlic, mustard and vinegar or lemon juice together in a bowl to combine. Now start to add the oils in a thin trickle, whisking constantly. When the oil starts to emulsify with the yolks you can add it a little faster. If things have gone to plan you will have a thick, glossy, garlicky mayonnaise. If it's too thick add 1 tbsp warm water to loosen it slightly. Cover and set aside until ready to serve.

Take the lobsters from the freezer and dispatch them quickly: put one on a large board with the head towards you and insert the tip of a sharp, heavy knife into the cross at the top of the lobster's head. Press down firmly, cutting through the head towards you. Repeat with the second lobster.

Using heavy-duty tongs or a spade, place half the hot bricks or stones in the base of the pit (pic 1) and quickly lay half the damp seaweed over the stones to make a deep, steamy nest (pic 2). Nestle in the lobsters, side by side (pic 3), cover with the remaining seaweed and lay the rest of the hot bricks on top (pic 4). Cover with earth (or shingle if you're on the beach) and leave for an hour to cook.

When the time is up, carefully remove the earth or shingle (pic 5) and stones to reveal the seaweed. Gather this up (it'll be hot), trying to keep the lobsters beneath quite clean, and hoik it out of the way. Lift the lobsters out of the pit (pic 6) and rinse to clean if necessary.

Place one lobster on a board with the tail facing you and use a large, heavy knife to cut centrally from the split in the head down though to the tip of the tail in one firm motion, so you end up with two even halves. Repeat with the second lobster. Use the back of the knife to crack the claws then bring everything to the table (if there is one). Serve with lemon wedges, aïoli, good bread and a green salad.

The Wood Oven

I was in my early twenties when I started working with

Hugh, while he was turning an old Dorset dairy farm outside the market town of Bridport into the first incarnation of River Cottage HQ. Hugh's approach to cooking was quite different from most of the conventional techniques I was used to and, for me, it was an exciting, experimental time. It was here that I really began cooking with fire.

Among the first things we built at HQ was a pair of large clay wood-burning ovens, which we sited just outside the kitchen door. They weren't the prettiest things to look at, but they had a certain rough-edged charm and, more importantly, they worked brilliantly. I'd never cooked in anything like them before, so I learned as I went along. I discovered that they were incredibly versatile: you could use them to cook really quickly when they were ferociously hot; or, when they were cooler, cook things in a much more gentle way over longer periods of time.

Soon I was using these rustic outdoor ovens in pretty much the same way as I would employ a conventional oven in the kitchen. Although I couldn't adjust the temperature with the turn of a dial, the more I cooked with them, the better I understood their unique qualities and the best ways to use them.

When the ovens were really hot I could, of course, turn out a mean pizza, with a crisp base, charred edges and bubbling, blistered topping. But, in addition, I'd roast fish until the skin puffed and cracked and turned from silver to gold, or sear steaks at 400°C until the fat crackled and spat and the meat began to smoke. I'd cook scallops in pools of bubbling butter and garlic, bake loaves of all shapes and sizes, and roast partridge and pigeon a dozen at a time. Apple tarts could be baked directly on the oven floor, puffing up the pastry in a way I hadn't seen before. In the autumn, I cooked vegetables – squash, beetroot and onions – with handfuls of herbs, to make into salads and soups. In the winter I'd braise venison and bacon together for hours on end, or slow-cook lamb at a very gentle heat while I went home and slept. Then, in the morning, I'd dry fruit, mushrooms and herbs in the remnants of the oven's warmth.

Ever since then, wood-burning ovens have played an invaluable part in the daily activities of the River Cottage kitchen. Each and every oven we've had has been a little different from the others, but they all work on the same principle.

How it works

Most wood-fired ovens are made of clay, brick, concrete or cob (a mixture of clay and straw) and have a domed interior. Unlike modern domestic ovens, where electricity or gas provides a constant regular heat, a wood oven is usually heated to a high temperature with an initial, fierce 'firing', after which it's not always necessary to keep the fire alight.

The fire is lit near to the front of the oven. Once it has taken hold and is burning well it's usually pushed to the back or to one side of the chamber. Throughout the firing period, the walls and floor of the oven heat up, slowly but surely – some ovens can reach temperatures in excess of 500°C. They then act like a thermal battery, slowly releasing the heat they have absorbed back into the oven space for hours, or even days. Wood ovens are highly insulated so that even after the fire has gone out, the oven will hold its heat.

The domed shape of the oven helps distribute heat pretty evenly. Nevertheless, as long as a fire is still burning within, it is likely to be the greatest heat source – this means you'll need to turn and adjust the position of the food as it's cooking.

As with most ovens, wood ovens cook partly by radiant heat, as waves of thermal energy travel through the oven space. But cooking by conduction – the direct

transfer of heat from one material to another – is also very important. In fact, it's one of the hallmarks of wood-oven cooking. The transfer of a tremendous amount of heat from the oven floor to the food that touches it produces rapid expansion, browning, crisping and charring. It's the reason that pizza works so well in this kind of oven: the oven floor can be holding upwards of 400°C heat, so as soon as a soft, light dough slides onto it, the direct heat transfer starts it swelling, crisping and charring incredibly quickly. Coupled with the radiant heat making the surface of the pizza melt and bubble, this results in a delicious outcome.

Convection – the flow of hot air – is another factor in wood-oven cooking. Cool air is constantly being sucked in through the open door of the oven and drawn towards the flames. Here it heats rapidly, travelling up and across the ceiling of the oven and down towards the flue and door. Hot air that doesn't escape is drawn down and sucked back round a second time. This cycle of hot air moving over and around the food contributes to even cooking.

Buying a wood oven

Anyone with a little space in their garden has the potential to own a wood-burning oven. I wanted one at home for years and now that I've finally got one I'd go as far as to say it's revolutionised my home cooking. I fire it up whenever I get the chance.

Off-the-shelf wood ovens come in all shapes and sizes. They're not particularly expensive, they're easy to install and, nine times out of ten, you can fire them up and get cooking almost straight away.

You can also buy more substantial ovens that come in kit form, which you assemble yourself. With these, you'll often need to make your own brick or hardwood plinth for the oven to sit on (see p.174). You may need to insulate the precast dome yourself, and render it too, and this gives you scope to be creative with your finishes. It's not uncommon to see conventionally shaped wood ovens finished in quirky ways – I've seen them styled as everything from a dragon to a pig's head. You may have a specific vision for how your wood oven fits in to the garden. Perhaps you want to house it in a wall or set it in a grassy bank, or within a more extensive outdoor-kitchen set-up.

Building your own wood oven

You can build your own wood oven from scratch. I've done it myself at River Cottage, as have hundreds of participants in the 'Build and Bake' courses held there; it is surprisingly achievable. You don't need any experience in bricklaying or building, and it's a job you can complete solo. I do think, however, that the help of a few handy friends makes the process much easier, not to mention more enjoyable. You can of course repay them in time with delicious wood-roasted food…

It will take 2–3 weeks, all in, before your oven is complete, but it only requires 3 days of actual work. And those are not consecutive days: the oven is built in three layers and each layer needs a few days' drying time before the next is added. Choose a period when you're as confident as you can be of reasonably dry, mild weather. Rainstorms or frosts will not do your nascent oven much good.

The site

It goes without saying that you cannot build an oven on shifting sands. You need solid, level, stable ground for the plinth on which your oven will sit. It's also essential that you leave enough space around the finished oven to enable you to stack some firewood and set up a table for ingredients, and enough space directly in front of it for you to stand and comfortably manoeuvre food in and out. Of course, you don't want your oven to be too near flammable things, such as wooden fences or overhanging trees. And consider the light too: it's quite likely that you'll use your oven more in the evening than at any other time of day, so you might prefer a site that catches the setting sun. At home, my garden oven is situated near my back door, close to the kitchen, which makes things very convenient.

The plinth

The igloo-like dome of your oven needs to sit on a raised plinth, between 1 metre and 1.5 metres from the ground. You must complete the plinth before you start on your oven, and it must be solid, sturdy and immovable. Building a good plinth is in fact more of a task than building the oven – but it will outlast the oven too. When the time comes, you'll be able to knock down the old oven and build a new one with no extra plinth-work involved.

At River Cottage, we built the frame of our plinth with railway sleepers. These were arranged to form a square 'box', three sleepers (70cm) high and 120cm square, and screwed together with brackets on the inside of the box. Sturdy wooden battens also work for this job. We filled the space inside the box with rubble, before topping it up with sand to a level one-brick's depth below the top of the sleepers. Fire bricks were set on top of the sand, fitted together as tightly as possible, to form the floor of the oven. A few gaps between bricks were filled with fireproof cement.

Alternatively you can make your plinth by building two breeze block uprights, spanned by reinforced concrete lintels onto which you bed your fire bricks. The benefit to this design is that it creates storage space underneath, which is perfect for logs and kindling (as shown on p.185).

The oven

The building of the oven itself breaks down into three stages, each dedicated to forming a separate layer of the oven: the inner 'skin', the insulating middle layer and the outer wall. You will need:

- **8 large buckets of clay** And I mean *large* – measure your clay with the kind of bucket used by builders, farmers and horse-riders (around 15 litre capacity). At River Cottage we dig our clay from a man-made pond on the farm. It is nice, moist clay and easy to work with: flexible enough to roll into a long sausage then wrap around a finger without snapping. Dry, crumbly clay is best avoided, as is clay mixed with a lot of earth, sticks or stones. You may have a source of good damp clay from a pond or stream on your property. Should you want to dig clay from land that isn't yours, you must have the landowner's permission. Alternatively, you can order clay from a builder's merchant or pottery supplier (see Directory, p.248).

- **18 large buckets of sand** Standard building sand is ideal. (If you decide to re-use some of the sand while you are building the oven, you may not need quite as much.)

- **2 carrier bags of wood shavings** I like mine to be roughly the texture of jumbo porridge oats! Timber merchants are your best bet.

- **A large, heavy-duty tarpaulin** Obtainable from DIY suppliers. Avoid anything flimsy, as it will need to withstand some rough treatment.

- **Newspaper** Just one should do it.

- **A thin stick** This will be used for measuring the thickness of your oven walls as you build them, so it needs to be thin enough to poke into soft clay. A strong but slender stick of 30cm or so, such as a kebab stick or knitting needle, is what you're after. Use a knife or a pen to mark a depth of 7cm at one end of it.

- **A long knife** You'll use this to cut the doorway.

- **10–12 bricks** These will form the door arch of the oven. Obtain from a builders' merchant, unless you have leftover bricks from another project.

First work day

Today you will be building a 'former' – a temporary dome made of sand, around which your oven will be shaped. Over this, you'll apply a clay-and-sand skin, which will be the inner surface of the oven, then you will remove the sand from inside. The skin needs to be left to dry after this, a process you should expedite by lighting your first fire inside the oven!

Mixing the clay and sand Lay the tarpaulin out on the ground and tip 6 buckets of sand and 3 buckets of clay onto it. Now you're going to mix the two together to form a malleable 'mud', using your feet. Wearing wellies, stomp all over the sand and clay, working them together. Periodically use the edges of the tarpaulin to lift and fold the mix over on itself. Keep doing this for up to 20 minutes. Pick out and discard any stones you come across on the way. If the mix seems dry and difficult to work with, add some water – just a little at a time.

You are aiming for a final consistency that is flexible but not floppy, so that you can mould it easily into shape and it will stay there. To test the consistency, take a fat nugget of the mix, about the size of a lime, and spend a minute or so compacting it thoroughly into a ball. Now hold out your hand at shoulder height and drop the ball onto the ground. It should crack but more or less hold its shape. If it 'splats' and flattens, it's too wet and you need a bit more sand in the mix. If it crumbles apart, it's too sandy and requires more clay. Adjust your mix if necessary and keep stomping and turning until you have the consistency right.

Building the former Trace a circle 80cm in diameter in the centre of your plinth. Now heap sand (just pure sand, not your clay-and-sand mix) into the middle of the circle. Form the sand into a dome. It shouldn't be a perfect hemisphere – you want the wall of the dome to rise vertically in a straight line for the first 8–10cm or so (roughly a hand-width) before it starts to curve inwards to the peak of the dome. The straighter your walls are the more internal space the oven will have.

As you're forming this former, stop every now and then and stand on the edge of the plinth, looking directly down over it. This is the best vantage point for spotting imperfections and lopsidedness.

At its highest point, the finished dome should be about 40cm high.

Papering the former When you are completely happy with the size and shape of your sand dome, you need to cover it with a layer of wet newspaper. When you come to dig out the sand later on, this paper layer will tell you when you've reached the inner wall of the oven.

Soak whole sheets of newspaper in water and lay them over the dome, patting them down over each other, until the dome is completely covered.

Papering the former
A cross-section is shown for illustrative purposes

Building the inner skin You are now going to cover the paper-clad dome with a thick layer of the clay-and-sand mixture. This 'inner skin' needs to be about 7cm deep and it's important that you compact the mixture as you go, eliminating air pockets, which would expand on heating and possibly cause cracks.

Start by taking a large handful of the clay-and-sand mix. Pat it into a rough brick shape and sit it against the base of your dome. Now hold one hand against the outside of the 'brick' and use the side of your other hand to knock the brick down, compacting it into a squat shape, around 7cm deep – i.e. from the dome to the outer edge of the 'brick', where your hand is. Use your measuring stick to check this depth. Repeat with a second 'brick' of clay-and-sand mix, butting it right up against the first, compacting it down, measuring the depth and then merging and moulding it together with the first brick. You shouldn't be able to see the join between them.

Continue like this all around the base of the oven, then begin a second row of clay-and-sand, above the first, working your way up towards the top of the dome. Measure the depth of the clay and check the dome from above periodically, as before. Once you've reached the top of the dome and closed the gap, depth-check the inner skin layer by poking your stick into it in several different places. Smooth it as much as possible: the more even the structure, the stronger it will be.

Building the inner skin

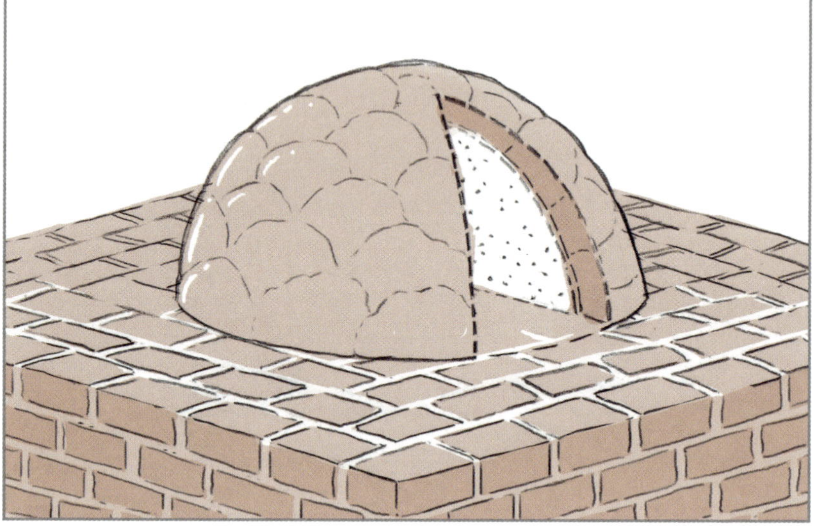

Removing the sand former

Once the inner skin layer is complete, sprinkle the remaining clay-and-sand mix with a little water and scoop it into some sturdy bin bags to keep it moist. You will need it on the second work day.

Now leave your dome for at least 2 hours to firm up before you come back for the next task.

Removing the sand former Use your long knife to cut an arch shape through the inner skin of your dome, where you want the oven door to be. As a guide, it should be about 30cm wide and 20cm high, but please consider the actual tins, trays or pizza peels that you will be using with your oven – you must be able to get them through this door!

Carefully pull away the clay-and-sand piece from the doorway you have just cut. Now use your hand to scoop out all the sand from inside the dome and discard it (or else re-combine it with the unused sand to avoid waste). As you work, be careful not to press your arm against the doorway, as this can squash it out of shape. Eventually, your hand inside the dome will reach the newspaper layer. When all the sand is out, carefully peel off and pull out the newspaper too.

Drying out the inner skin (4–6 days)

The clay-and-sand mix is firm but still damp at this point. Over the next few days you need to let it dry out completely. Begin by just leaving the inner skin to dry naturally for about 48 hours. Then light a fire inside the oven to help complete the drying process.

Begin – as you will do when you are using your oven 'for real' – by lighting the fire at the front of the oven by the doorway. The greater amount of oxygen here will help it catch. When it is burning well, push the fire back into the oven with an ash rake or similar tool (see p.188). At first, your fire may struggle inside the damp dome, but persevere, starting again if you have to.

When the fire gets going inside, you will see steam rising from moist clay. Let the fire burn, feeding it periodically, for 2–3 hours. Then allow it to go out and let the oven continue to dry on its own for at least a couple of days, protecting it with a tarpaulin if it rains.

The oven is ready when it feels dry to the touch and is noticeably lighter in colour all over. I would expect this first drying stage to take a maximum of 6 days – less in warm weather.

Second work day

Once the inner skin of the oven is dry, your next tasks are to build the brick door arch, form a simple chimney and apply the insulating layer of the oven.

Building the door arch Return to your buckets of sand – you are going to make another former, this time for the little 'tunnel' that will lead from the outside of the oven to the inside. Heap some sand in front of the oven doorway. Mould the sand into an arched shape, coming forward from the door. The 'arch' should follow the door's shape and extend one brick's length, at the base, from the oven wall.

Build an arch around this sand former with your bricks, using some of the clay-and-sand mix that you set aside as mortar. There will be a gap between the top bricks and the wall of the oven, where the dome recedes. Fill this gap with more of the clay-and-sand, forming a 'collar' between the brick arch and the oven itself.

Cutting and forming the chimney Using your knife again, cut a hole, about 20cm in diameter, in the section of clay at the top of the collar, and remove the disc of clay from the hole. Use more clay-and-sand to build a little chimney rising up from this hole, about 20cm high (by moulding 'sausages' of the mix into rings and layering them up, melding the rings together as you go). Alternatively, you can fit a short length of flue pipe to the hole or up-cycle an existing terracotta chimney pot. You could even knock the bottom off an old flower pot and use that instead. Leave for at least a couple of hours so this fresh section of clay settles and firms up, then scoop out the sand from inside your newly built door arch, as you did before.

Mixing a 'slip' This is done by thinning down some clay-and-sand with water to form a sloppy mixture. In the absence of industrial tools, mixing by foot, on the tarpaulin with your wellies on, is the simplest option. But you can mix by hand if you prefer, in a large vessel such as a dustbin. Either way, combine one bucket of clay with about half a bucket of warm water. Now mix the two together – by foot or by hand. Add more water as you go, until you have what is technically known as a 'sludgy gloop' with the consistency of yoghurt. This is your slip.

Now add your 2 carrier bags of wood shavings to the slip and mix them in until thoroughly combined.

Building the insulating layer Build a layer of this slip-and-shavings mix over your oven, in exactly the same way you did with the first layer of clay-and-sand. Use the same method, forming 'bricks' of mixture, tamping them down to compact them, and melding them together. You want the same depth of 7cm all over – so use your measuring stick again. Take the mixture up to the point where the door arch juts away from the oven – you don't need to cover the brick arch or the chimney.

Building the door arch

Building the insulating layer

Building the outer wall

The finished oven

Drying out the insulating layer (4–6 days)

As before, this layer needs to dry out completely over the next few days. Follow the method and timings suggested on p.179 for drying the first layer, lighting a fire inside the oven after a couple of days to hasten the drying process.

Third work day

Things are getting exciting now. Your final task is to build the outer wall of the oven. Then you just have to wait for this layer to dry before you can fire up your oven and start cooking.

Building the outer wall This is simply a repeat of building the inner skin – same materials, same method. So mix up 4 buckets of clay and 8 buckets of sand on your tarpaulin (in the way you did on the first work day) and crack on!

Don't cover the bricks of the doorway arch but do cover the chimney in a layer of clay-and-sand, slightly shallower than that over the main body of the oven. This will be the final, visible outer layer of your oven so take your time getting it as smooth and neat as possible, using wet hands and a wettened trowel.

Drying out the outer wall (4–6 days)

Let the outer skin dry, as before, using a fire to help speed the process.

De-sanding

One important final step is to clear any residual sand out of the inside of the oven. You can do this with a brush – a special pizza oven brush with stiff metal bristles is ideal. But in order to be sure of getting rid of any last annoying grains of sand, I wouldn't be above getting a hoover nozzle in there.

You are now ready to start cooking!

Final touches

If you're handy with a jigsaw, you could make a removable wooden door and chimney cover for the oven. These are not essential, but they do allow you to minimise heat loss from the oven, prolonging cooking time. They must not be used when there are flames in the oven; wait until the fire dies down to glowing embers.

For these finishing touches, you'll need a piece of wood 2–3cm thick. From it, cut pieces to fit the doorway and the chimney opening. You will need to fix some kind of handle to both – just another small piece of wood, screwed or nailed on will suffice. It's a good idea to soak these wooden covers in water before each use, to help stop them warping.

Looking after your oven

After each use, brush your oven out thoroughly once it has cooled down, in order to get rid of ash and burnt scraps of food.

When you are not using the oven, it's essential that you protect it from the elements. A tarpaulin is the simplest, though perhaps not the most aesthetic option. Some people prefer to build a little roof structure over the oven. If you do this, don't build the roof too low or it will trap smoke – at least a metre's clearance between oven and roof is ideal.

As you use your wood oven, you may see some cracking start to appear on the outer surface. This isn't a significant issue unless the cracks start to become large or deep – in which case they will allow heat to escape. Simply fill in any worrying cracks with clay.

An oven like this is not designed to last forever. Created from the earth itself and standing outside in fluctuating temperatures and humidity, it will, one day, start to crumble. But a well-built example, protected from the worst of the weather, should last at least 5 years – quite possibly more. And the great thing is that when your oven does reach the end of its useful life, you can simply knock it down with a hefty sledgehammer and start again!

Cooking in the oven

As with most things in life, practice makes perfect. Each oven will have its own character and unique foibles. The more fires you light in it and the more things you cook in it, the more familiar you'll become with how it works and how to get the best from it.

I find that I learn the most by simply watching. I watch the fire take, watch it build, watch the flames grow and how they tumble and roll. I watch how one wood burns compared to another. I watch the smoke and its colour. I watch the ceiling for signs that the oven has heated up properly (i.e. when the black char there has disappeared and the oven has 'burned clean'). Most importantly, I watch how the food is cooking.

Firing up the oven

Lighting a wood oven is easy. You just need to build a small fire at the entrance to the oven using the basic technique described on pp.26–30. (If you really feel the need for firelighters, use natural ones – petroleum-based firelighters smell horrible and will taint your food.) Occasionally, when the oven is particularly cold or damp, or hasn't been lit for a long time, it can be difficult to light. This is due to negative

pressure from cold air, which can effectively block the chimney. This suppresses the fire and causes excessive smoking. But as long as your kindling is bone dry, the fire will soon take hold and warm the flue. I tend to set the fire near the doorway of the oven. This is partly for practical reasons (it's easier to reach) but also because the free-flowing air at the entrance aids combustion.

Once the fire is going, it's all too tempting to pile larger pieces of wood on at once. But it's better to keep to small pieces initially. The smaller they are, the quicker and hotter they will burn. This gets the oven hot, which will make it much easier for larger pieces of wood to catch later on.

Once the fire is established and some heat has built up, the next step is to push the burning wood to the back of the oven. Resist the urge to do this before the fire is really going strong, because disturbing the fire too early can set it back and even put it out. It's easiest to use a purpose-made tool – called an ash rake, or a fire rake – to push the fire to the back of the oven. But if you don't happen to possess one of these, a small garden rake will do the trick.

Once you've created space at the front of the oven by pushing back the fire, you might want to put some extra wood near the front to heat up. This dries the wood further and eventually it will get so hot it will be near combustion. When this wood is finally pushed into the fire at the back, it ignites easily and produces heat quickly. It's a tip that's worth remembering – particularly if your wood is a little under-seasoned or green.

The fire generally needs to burn for between 45 and 90 minutes in order to get the oven up to cooking temperature. But this is only a guide and a good deal depends on the conditions on any particular day. If the oven is damp and cold to start with and the weather chilly, it may take well over an hour to heat. By contrast, on a dry, hot summer's day, or if the oven was used only the night before, it could be ready to cook within 20 minutes. One rule of thumb is that any initial sooty deposits on the ceiling of the oven will have burnt away by the time the oven is hot enough to cook in.

General cooking advice

Knowing exactly when to start cooking depends on what you are intending to cook. A lot of wood-oven cooking is about high heat and quick results, but these ovens are also good for slower, gentler, more regulated cooking.

In all instances, it's best to hold off putting your food into the oven until you are absolutely sure it's at the right temperature. A pizza cooked in a sluggish oven won't be the same as one cooked in a raging inferno. Likewise, a chicken or a joint of pork cooked at scorching heat will be black on the outside long before it's cooked in the middle. But this is no different from cooking in your domestic oven: get the temperature right and usually things turn out well.

Unlike a regular oven, however, you can't turn a wood oven down – or up, for that matter. The only 'dial' is the wood you feed it with or, indeed, don't feed it with. Patience – lovely word – is required while the oven heats up or cools down, and you'll need to pay attention to ensure the food you're cooking is responding in the way you'd like it to. That means (as with nearly all forms of outdoor cooking) being there in person to monitor and to adjust anything and everything that might need it. Perhaps the fire needs feeding or evening out, or the food needs rotating, covering or uncovering. Or, if the oven door is in place (because you have removed the fire), it might need opening. If you're not there, you'll never know.

In a small oven, it can make sense to remove the embers before you put any food in to cook, particularly if it's a lot of food. The fire will have done its job of heating the oven, and you don't want the fire to scorch the food closest to it in the limited space. Use an ash rake to scrape the hot embers towards the mouth of the oven, and a metal shovel or dustpan to transfer them to a metal dustbin to cool. (Once cool, a handful of these ashes and embers can be added to your compost heap from time to time. They are a source of potassium and are alkaline, which makes them useful for correcting an acidic soil. However, you shouldn't over-use wood ash in the garden, as many plants don't thrive in an alkaline environment.)

For a larger oven, you can keep the glowing embers in while you cook. In some cases – say if you wanted to cook lots of batches of pizza over an extended period of time – you'll need to maintain a very high heat in the oven by feeding the fire with dry wood several times over the cooking period.

For a recipe that requires longer, more gentle cooking – a shoulder of lamb, for example – the heat already built up in the oven should be enough. But you should check the temperature of the oven periodically with an oven thermometer, and feed the fire to raise the temperature if necessary. It's possible you'll have to re-fire the oven if you have removed the fire and the temperature has dropped to low, but I'd recommend keeping a small fire burning throughout long, slow cooking if you can.

Lots of wood ovens have thermometers set into the door, so that when the door is closed, you'll have a fairly good idea of the temperature inside. You can also buy small oven thermometers that sit somewhere in the oven itself to tell you the temperature in that area. A more sophisticated way of getting accurate readings is to use an infrared point-and-shoot thermometer. This will give you an exact reading of any particular surface you aim it at and is perfect for gauging the heat of the oven floor.

When a fire's going really well, the temperature can be several hundred degrees higher at the ceiling than on the floor, so the height of the oven will have a bearing on how things cook.

In the end, it's all worth it. Food from a wood oven has been the basis for some of the best meals I've ever had.

Essential kit for the wood oven

- **Trays and dishes** For roasting or stewing in your wood oven, choose robust, heavy-bottomed metal roasting trays or cast-iron casseroles. Avoid thin metal cookware that will buckle or twist in the oven's intense heat.

- **Pizza peel** When it comes to sliding pizza or bread dough into the raging heart of the wood oven, a purpose-made 'peel' (a flat metal paddle on a long handle) is extremely useful. A quick back-and-forth shoving movement from you will shoot the pizza onto the scorching oven floor. However, you can also bake pizza and bread on a sturdy baking sheet. A pizza wheel is useful too, for cutting pizzas into slices effortlessly.

- **Ash rake** Also called a fire rake, this simple, long-handled tool will enable you to push a fire deeper into the oven, as well as scrape embers or ash out again.

- **Metal dustbin** A sturdy metal bin is the ideal receptacle for hot embers scraped out of the oven.

- **Oven brush** A purpose-made brush, with stiff wire bristles and a long handle, makes it easy to clean the oven floor once it's cooled down.

- **Fireproof gloves** A pair of these, or even just one, will save you a lot of burnt fingers.

- **Tarpaulin** It is a good idea to have something with which to protect your wood oven from the elements when it's not in use, especially during the winter. You will need to secure the tarp over the oven with weights or rope.

Pizza dough

Some people call all wood-fired ovens 'pizza ovens'. While this glosses over their extraordinary versatility, I can see why. Pizza is, without question, the single most popular thing to cook in a wood oven and for good reason.

Pizza, in general, has become a victim of its own success; it's been commodified – as have so many of the things we love to eat. The worst offenders are nothing more than fat, salt, sugar, highly processed wheat and E numbers. But homemade pizza, cooked in a wood-burning oven, is the antithesis of this kind of travesty. From the dough up, you have complete control. You can cover your base with fresh, ripe tomatoes, a vibrant homemade pesto, or soft, sweet caramelised onions. You can finish your pizza with a silky, milky buffalo mozzarella or a salty, crumbly mature Cheddar. You can create something that's not only delicious but that can also, I think, be considered good for you (all things in moderation).

A DIY pizza night at home is one of my favourite things, and that's not just because the pizza is delicious. It's also a creative, communal and inclusive event. Everyone feels part of the fun and can pick and choose whatever they fancy to go on their pizza before experiencing the thrill of baking it themselves in the awesome heat of the roaring oven. I put the dough together in the morning, light the oven in the afternoon then, as the sun falls in the sky, we all get together to make and bake our pizzas. I'll throw together a couple of salads, and we'll have some good wine too, but those are the only accompaniments needed.

You can make your basic pizza dough using dried yeast, or you can try a sourdough version with a fermenting leaven, or 'starter'. Making sourdough is slightly more involved – you'll need to have an active starter on the go and get the dough made up in advance – but it doesn't really take any longer. You'll notice a difference in the texture of the crust and crumb, which will be robust and deliciously chewy, with a subtly sour flavour.

P.S. If you don't have an active sourdough starter to hand, you'll need to allow 5 days to make one. Place 25g rye flour and 50ml warm water in a clean bowl, stir well, cover and leave overnight in a warm place (around 30°C). The next day, add 25g rye flour and 50ml warm water, stir well, cover and return the mixture to the warm place. Repeat on the third and fourth day (it should show signs of fermentation on day 3). On the fifth day you should have 300g or so of active starter. Store in the fridge, feeding it once or twice more, with 25g rye flour and 50ml warm water each time, to ensure it is active before you use it. Every time you use some of the starter, replace with an equal weight of flour and water mix (1 part flour to 2 parts water).

Sourdough pizza dough

For 2 large pizzas

50g active sourdough starter
   (see left)
160ml water
250g strong white bread flour

5g salt
A little oil, for oiling
Extra flour or fine semolina,
   for dusting

Put the starter and water into a large bowl, add the flour and salt, mix to a rough dough, then turn out onto a clean surface and knead by hand for 7–10 minutes, or knead in a mixer fitted with the dough hook for about 5 minutes until the dough feels soft, stretchy and smooth; if it feels too sticky, add a shake more flour.

Wipe out the bowl and lightly oil it, then return the dough to it, cover with a cloth and leave to rise at room temperature for 2½ hours.

Lightly dust a tray with flour or semolina. Tip the risen dough out onto a clean surface and divide in two. Loosely shape each piece into a ball and place both on the prepared tray. Give the top of the dough a light scattering of flour or semolina too. Loosely cover the dough balls with cling film or a cloth and place in the fridge. This dough will be good to use after an hour's proving but will hold well in the fridge for up to 24 hours.

Standard pizza dough

For 2 large pizzas

250g strong white bread flour
3g fast-action dried yeast
5g salt
170ml water

A little oil, for oiling
Extra flour or fine semolina,
   for dusting

In a large bowl, mix the flour, yeast, salt and water to a rough dough. Turn out onto a clean surface and knead by hand for 7–10 minutes, or knead in a mixer fitted with the dough hook for about 5 minutes until the dough feels soft, stretchy and smooth.

Wipe out the bowl and lightly oil it, then return the dough to it, cover with a cloth and leave to rise at room temperature for an hour.

Lightly dust a tray with flour or semolina. Tip the risen dough out onto a clean surface and divide in two. Loosely shape each piece into a ball and place both balls on the prepared tray. Give the tops a dusting of flour or semolina too. Leave to rest at room temperature for 20 minutes before using.

Onion and kale pizza
with mozzarella and anchovies

I've been making this autumnal-tasting pizza for years because it's just so good: sweet from the onions, salty from the anchovies, rich from the cheese, with a kind of 'crisp around the edges texture' from the kale. Sometimes I like to add a healthy scattering of dried chilli flakes before it goes in the oven.

Makes 2 large pizzas

1 quantity pizza dough (pp.190–1)
Fine semolina or polenta, for dusting

For the topping
2 small onions, peeled and finely sliced
Olive oil, for cooking
2 handfuls of tender kale

12 anchovy fillets in oil
1 large ball of buffalo mozzarella, torn into pieces
50g Cheddar, coarsely grated
Sea salt and freshly ground black pepper

Pre-fire your wood oven (see pp.184–7). It should be around 350°C when you start to cook.

Put the onions into an ovenproof heavy-based frying pan, toss them with a little olive oil, sea salt and pepper and transfer the pan to a medium-hot area of the wood oven. Cook for 20–30 minutes until they are soft and have taken on a little colour, stirring them regularly and ensuring they don't burn.

Meanwhile, take the kale off its stalks and tear it into little pieces. Once the onions are soft, add the kale to the pan and return to the oven. The heat of the oven should soften the kale very quickly. Set aside while you prepare the pizza bases.

Sprinkle your work surface with a little semolina or polenta. Place one ball of dough on the surface and stretch it out by hand to a large round, 25–30cm in diameter, leaving a little ridge around the edge. Repeat with the second piece of dough.

Dust a pizza peel with more polenta or semolina (if you don't have a peel, an upturned baking tray is a good substitute). Transfer one pizza base to it.

Top the pizza with half the onion and kale mix, anchovies, mozzarella and grated Cheddar. Finish with a drizzle of olive oil. Gently slide the pizza onto the base of the oven. Depending on the heat of the oven, it will take between 3 and 5 minutes until the base is cooked, the cheese is bubbling away and the kale is nice and crispy. Slide the pizza out of the oven then assemble and bake the second pizza.

Seafood pizza
with mussels and cockles

This is an incredibly delicious seafood pizza. I use live mussels and cockles or clams in the shell; they open in the high heat of the wood oven and spill their juices onto the pizza, giving it an amazing flavour. The result is so rich and full of character that you really don't need cheese – although anything goes, of course.

Makes 2 large pizzas

1 quantity pizza dough (pp.190–1)
Fine semolina or polenta, for dusting
Sea salt and freshly ground
  black pepper

For the tomato sauce

1 tbsp olive oil
1 garlic clove, peeled and finely
  grated
2 bay leaves
400g tin chopped tomatoes
A good pinch of sugar

For the topping

About 16 live mussels
About 16 live cockles or clams
  (or use more mussels)
About 300g cooked white fish,
  such as sustainably caught pollack,
  whiting, cod or haddock
4 garlic cloves, peeled and finely sliced
A small bunch of parsley, finely
  chopped
A handful of fennel fronds, chopped
Extra virgin olive oil, to trickle

Pre-fire your wood oven (see pp.184–7). It should be around 350°C when you start to cook.

To make the tomato sauce, set a small pan over a medium heat. Add the olive oil, followed by the grated garlic and bay leaves. As soon as the garlic is beginning to sizzle, add the chopped tomatoes, sugar and a little salt and pepper. Half-fill the empty tomato tin with water and pour this in too. Cook gently for 20–30 minutes or until the sauce is thick and pulpy. Remove from the heat and allow to cool.

Meanwhile, prepare the shellfish. Put them all into a colander and rinse thoroughly under a running cold tap. If any of the shells are open, give them a sharp tap against the side of the sink. If the shells do not close, it indicates that particular shellfish is dead and you should discard it. Check over the mussels and pull away any little wiry 'beards' attached to the shells.

Sprinkle your work surface with a little semolina or polenta. Stretch out one ball of dough on the surface by hand to a large round, 25–30cm in diameter, leaving a little ridge around the edge. Repeat with the second piece of dough.

Dust a pizza peel with polenta or semolina (if you don't have a peel, an upturned baking tray is a good substitute). Transfer one pizza base to it.

Top the pizza with half the tomato sauce. Break the white fish into big chunks and dot half on to the pizza, then add half the mussels and cockles or clams. Scatter over half the sliced garlic and season all over with salt and pepper.

Slide the pizza into the wood oven and cook for 5–8 minutes. It is done when the base is golden, the shellfish have opened up nicely (discard any that refuse to open), and the sauce is bubbling. Slide the pizza out of the oven and finish with a final trickle of olive oil and a scattering of chopped parsley and fennel fronds. Assemble and bake the second pizza. Eat straight away, discarding the shells as you prise the morsels of shellfish from them.

Wild mushroom pizza
with Parmesan, truffle oil and chives

I make this pizza every year when wild mushrooms come into season – it's such a treat. You can use cultivated mushrooms, but the deep, bosky flavour of certain foraged mushrooms takes some beating. Ceps and hedgehogs are my favourites.

Makes 2 large pizzas

1 quantity pizza dough (pp.190–1)
Fine polenta or semolina, for dusting

For the topping
A knob of butter
3 tbsp extra virgin olive oil
2 large onions, peeled, halved and
    thinly sliced
4 garlic cloves, peeled and chopped

2 sprigs of thyme, leaves picked
100g Parmesan, finely grated
250g wild or cultivated mushrooms,
    sliced
A small bunch of chives, finely sliced
2–3 tsp good truffle oil
Sea salt and freshly ground
    black pepper

Pre-fire your wood oven (see pp.184–7). It should be around 350°C when you come to cook.

Place a large, heavy-based pan over a medium heat. Add the butter and 1 tbsp extra virgin olive oil. When it's bubbling away, add the onions, along with a good pinch of salt and some black pepper. Cook, stirring regularly, for 15–20 minutes or until the onions are soft and just beginning to caramelise at their edges. Stir in the garlic and thyme and cook for 3–4 minutes longer. Set to one side.

Sprinkle your work surface with a little polenta or semolina. Place one ball of dough on the surface and stretch out by hand to a round, 25–30cm in diameter. Repeat with the second piece of dough.

Dust a pizza peel with polenta or semolina (if you don't have a peel, an upturned baking tray is a good substitute). Transfer one pizza base to it. Arrange half the onions over the pizza base and then sprinkle over a quarter of the Parmesan. Lay half the mushrooms over the cheese, trickle with 1 tbsp extra virgin olive oil and season with salt and pepper. Scatter over another quarter of the Parmesan, followed by a small handful of finely chopped chives.

Slide the pizza into the wood oven and cook for 3–5 minutes or until crisp, golden and bubbling. Remove the pizza to a plate or board, and trickle over the truffle oil. Assemble and bake the second pizza.

Coco's garlic bread

Whenever we make pizzas and bake them in the wood oven, my daughter Coco likes to make these garlic breads as well. They are her speciality and they're very good. Sometimes she pushes the boat out and covers them with grated Cheddar too. For this recipe, you will need to divide the risen pizza dough into four before shaping into balls.

Makes 4 large garlic breads
2 quantities pizza dough (pp.190–1)
Fine polenta or semolina, for dusting
4 sprigs of thyme, leaves picked
Sea salt and freshly ground
    black pepper

For the garlicky butter
8 garlic cloves, peeled
180g unsalted butter, softened
A bunch of parsley, leaves picked
    and chopped

Pre-fire your wood oven (see pp.184–7). It should be about 350°C when you come to bake.

For the garlicky butter, grate the garlic using a fine grater such as a Microplane, or crush it to a coarse paste. Mix with the butter, parsley and some salt and pepper.

Sprinkle your work surface with a little semolina or polenta. Place one ball of dough on the surface and stretch it out by hand to a round (or square), 25–30cm in diameter, leaving a ridge around the edge which will puff up nicely in the oven. Alternatively, use a rolling pin. Repeat with the other three pieces of dough.

Dust a pizza peel with more polenta or semolina (if you don't have a peel, an upside-down baking tray is a good substitute). Transfer one piece of dough to it.

Spread a quarter of the garlicky butter over the dough and finish with a grinding of black pepper and some thyme leaves. Slide the dough into the wood oven and keep an eye on it. It will need 2–5 minutes to turn golden brown and crisp on the base, depending on the heat. Repeat with the remaining dough and garlic butter.

Rosemary focaccia
with chorizo and goat's cheese

The combination of spicy chorizo, soft goat's cheese and aromatic rosemary turns this classic Italian bread into a meal. I often serve it with sliced tomatoes dressed with red wine vinegar and olive oil, a crunchy green salad, and a few cold beers.

Serves 4–6

For the dough
500g strong white bread flour
425ml water
5g fast-action dried yeast
10g salt
A little olive oil, for oiling
Fine polenta or semolina, for dusting

For the topping
100g cured chorizo
75g soft goat's cheese
4 large sprigs of rosemary, leaves
   picked
Sea salt

Put the flour, water, yeast and salt into a large bowl and combine to form a very soft, almost batter-like dough. Tip the dough out onto a clean surface.

Drizzle a little olive oil over your hands and begin to knead the dough. It's a very wet dough, which may feel unusual at first, but it will result in a light and bubbly focaccia. To knead, I find it is easiest to lift the dough up and slap it back down on the work surface, stretching the dough as you do so. After about 5–7 minutes of this process, the dough should begin to feel nice and stretchy. Wipe out the bowl and lightly oil it. Transfer the dough to the bowl, cover with cling film or a cloth and leave to rise at room temperature for 1½ hours.

About an hour before the dough finishes rising, light up your wood oven (see pp.184–7). It should be about 300°C when you come to bake.

Drizzle a baking tray with olive oil and dust it with a little polenta. Drizzle a little more oil over your hands. Lift the dough very gently from the bowl onto the tray, gently encouraging it to fill the entire space.

Slice the chorizo and dot it over the focaccia. Break up the cheese into chunks and press these into the surface of the dough then scatter with rosemary leaves. Give the surface a generous drizzle of olive oil and transfer the focaccia to the hot wood oven. It should take around 15 minutes to bake at this moderate heat – but do keep checking and turning the tray to ensure the bread doesn't start to catch.

Turn out the focaccia on to a wire rack and leave to cool a little before you tuck in.

Wood-roast sardines
with herbs and garlic

In a perfect world, I think sardines would always be served with crisp, golden skins. This means cooking them for a short time over a hot, hot fire or, better still, in a hot wood oven. The results are blistery, salty, garlicky, finger-licking good.

Serves 4

12 fresh sardines or Cornish pilchards
4 tbsp olive oil
2 tsp chopped marjoram
1 tsp chopped thyme

4 garlic cloves, peeled and sliced
Sea salt and freshly ground
  black pepper
Lemon wedges, to serve

Pre-fire your wood oven (see pp.184–7). It should be about 300°C when you come to cook.

Sardines have delicate flesh that will bruise and tear quite readily so be careful when preparing them for cooking. If they are not already prepared, use your thumb to rub off the large scales, and scissors to snip out the belly and guts and remove the fins. Wash the fish gently under the tap.

In a bowl, mix the olive oil with the herbs and garlic.

Place the sardines in a large roasting tray in a single layer, making sure they have a little space around them. Spoon the oil mixture over them, sprinkle generously with salt and pepper and turn to coat. Place the tray in the hot oven and cook the fish for 3–4 minutes until blistered and golden.

Remove the sardines from the tray and serve at once, with lemon wedges, good bread and a big green salad.

Whole roast brill
with fennel seeds, lemon and chilli

Brill is a sensational flat fish with firm white flesh and a great flavour – just as good as turbot, its more celebrated cousin. When you cook brill in the wood oven, its skin crisps, blisters and tears and it gets deliciously smoky. I love it with this butter – flavoured with fennel seeds, black pepper, chilli and lemon. As it melts, it finds its way into the fish, keeping it beautifully moist.

Serves 2

1 brill, 1–1.5kg, cleaned
Sea salt and freshly ground
    black pepper

For the flavoured butter
2 tsp fennel seeds
1 tsp black peppercorns
25g butter, softened
Grated zest of 1 lemon
½ tsp dried chilli flakes
2 garlic cloves, peeled and grated
A small handful of fennel fronds,
    chopped (optional)

Pre-fire your wood oven (see pp.184–7). It should be 200–250°C when you come to cook.

Put the fennel seeds and black peppercorns into a mortar and crush them coarsely with the pestle. Transfer to a bowl and mix with the butter, lemon zest, chilli flakes, garlic, chopped fennel fronds if using, and some salt and pepper.

Rub a small amount of the butter over the base of a large baking tray. Place the brill in the middle of the tray. Rub the top of the fish with the remaining fennel butter and season lightly with salt and pepper.

Place the tray in the wood oven and cook, rotating the tray once or twice, for 15 minutes, or until the fish flesh just comes away from the bone.

Remove the fish from the wood oven and serve at once, with new potatoes and a green salad.

Wood-roast chicken
with potatoes and herbs

This is a divine way to cook chicken and potatoes, and perfectly suited to the wood oven. The potatoes soak up all the rich juices from the chicken as it roasts, giving them an unbelievable flavour. You don't get gravy but you do get an extraordinary combination of deeply flavoured soft potatoes underneath a layer of crispy ones.

Serves 4

1 large free-range or organic chicken,
    about 2kg
60g butter, softened
4 sprigs of thyme, leaves picked
    and chopped
A small bunch of flat-leaf parsley,
    leaves picked and chopped
2 garlic cloves, peeled and grated

4 medium potatoes, about 1kg in total
10 bay leaves, roughly torn
2 tbsp olive oil
Sea salt and freshly ground
    black pepper

To serve
Aïoli (p.165)

Pre-fire your wood oven (see pp.184–7). It should be 200–220°C when you come to cook. An hour or so before you are ready to cook, take the chicken from the fridge and let it come up to room temperature.

Loosen the chicken breast skin a little, easing it away from the flesh with your fingers. Place the butter in a bowl and add the chopped thyme, parsley, garlic and some salt and pepper. Mix well to combine. Spread this herby butter under the breast skin and all over the surface of the chicken.

Peel the potatoes and finely slice into 4–5mm slices. Place in a large bowl with the torn bay leaves, olive oil and some salt and pepper and tumble together to coat.

Scatter the potatoes in a large roasting tray, in an even layer, and sit the chicken on top. Roast in the hot oven, turning the tray periodically, for about 1½ hours until the chicken and potatoes are cooked. Check the oven temperature from time to time; if it falls below about 120°C, build up the fire with fresh wood to keep it hot. To check whether the chicken is cooked, slide the tray to the front of the oven and pull at one of the legs – it should come away easily from the bird. Or use a digital probe thermometer in the thickest part (inside of the thigh, next to the body) to check the core temperature has reached 72°C. Remove from the oven once cooked.

Let the cooked meat and spuds rest for 15–20 minutes before carving and serving, with the aïoli and a crisp green salad.

Wood-roast pork belly
with apples and sage

I will never tire of roast pork with apples and sage; it reminds me of autumn and Sunday walks, falling leaves and homemade cider. A couple of tips for this recipe: take the pork out of its wrapping or bag and leave it uncovered, on a tray in the bottom of the fridge, for at least 24 hours before cooking. This helps to dry the skin to ensure better crackling. And be aware that crackling does have a tendency to burn in a wood oven, so keep a close eye on the pork in the initial stages.

Serves 4

A large piece of free-range or organic pork belly, about 1.5–2kg, skin scored
1 tbsp olive oil
4 eating apples
A large handful of sage leaves, roughly torn
Sea salt and freshly ground black pepper

Pre-fire your wood oven (see pp.184–7). It should be about 250°C when you start to cook.

An hour or so before you are ready to cook, take the pork belly from the fridge and let it come up to room temperature.

Place the pork belly, skin side up, on a medium baking tray. Rub it with the olive oil and season generously with salt and pepper. Place in the hot oven and cook for 15–30 minutes, rotating the tray regularly, until the pork skin puffs up and starts to crackle (leave it in for a bit longer if necessary), then take it out. (If it looks like it's going to burn before it has crackled, remove it from the oven anyway.)

Let the oven cool to about 180°C. Return the pork to the oven and cook for about 2 hours. Check the temperature of the oven from time to time and, if it falls below about 150°C, build up the fire with fresh wood to keep it hot.

Take the pork belly out of the oven. Halve the apples and place them, cut side down, on the baking tray to coat them in the pork fat, then turn them cut side up. Arrange the torn sage around the pork and apples and season the apples and sage with salt and pepper.

Return the pork belly to the oven and roast for a further 45 minutes to 1 hour, or until the meat is nice and tender and the apples are lovely and soft. Let it rest for at least 15 minutes before slicing and serving between thick slices of good bread.

Wood-roast lamb shoulder
cooked on a bed of dhal

This is one of the most delicious one-pot dishes you can imagine. Lamb tastes wonderful when it is cooked in the wood oven and the dhal soaks up all the flavourful meat juices as it cooks. Serve it with flatbreads and a tomato salad.

Serves 8

1 shoulder of lamb, about 2.5kg
Olive oil, for cooking
Sea salt and freshly ground
   black pepper

For the dhal

175g red lentils, rinsed
1 medium onion, peeled and sliced
4 garlic cloves, peeled and thinly sliced

1 dried red chilli, deseeded and
   finely sliced or crushed
1 litre well-flavoured veg stock
1½ tsp cumin seeds
1½ tsp black onion seeds
2 tsp curry powder
A pinch of dried curry leaves
1½ tsp tomato purée

Pre-fire your wood oven (see pp.184–7). It should be about 250°C when you start to cook.

An hour or so before you are ready to cook, take the lamb from the fridge and let it come up to room temperature.

Sit the lamb shoulder in a large, deep roasting tray. Trickle with 2 tbsp olive oil and season generously with salt and pepper. Place in the hot oven for 20–30 minutes so that it takes on some colour.

Take the roasting tray from the oven and lift the lamb shoulder out onto a plate. Add all the dhal ingredients to the tray, season well with salt and pepper and stir to combine. Set the lamb in the middle, nestling it in the dhal. Let the oven cool to 170–180°C then return the tray to it. Make sure the oven isn't too hot – the lamb needs to cook slowly now, over a period of 3–4 hours or more. Rotate the tray from time to time during cooking, checking the lamb and stirring the dhal at the same time. If the dhal looks too thick, loosen it with some hot water. Check the temperature of the oven occasionally and, if it falls below 150°C, build up the fire with fresh wood to keep it hot.

When the meat is tender, take the tray from the oven. Taste the dhal and adjust the seasoning, adding a splash of hot water if needed. Rest the meat for 15–20 minutes before carving and serving.

Spit-roasting

I've cooked a whole pig on a spit many times – and on every occasion, I cannot believe how much fun I have doing it. The meat is juicy, tender and smoky, and the crackling is almost invariably delectable. Served up in soft, floury baps with a spoonful of sweet apple sauce, it's such a treat. Moreover, spit-roasting is a brilliant way to bring people together and mark a celebration. And it doesn't have to be a pig – a whole lamb or several chickens are also fantastic cooked on the spit.

Spit-roasting differs from other forms of open-fire cooking in that, as the food is turned on the spit, it is exposed to a burst of intense heat from the fire, followed by a much cooler interval as it is turned away again. In addition, as the meat revolves on the spit, fat and juices are directed back inside it, rather than dripping out, so the meat is effectively self-basting.

How it works

Like many of the techniques discussed in this book, cooking meat on a spit or rotisserie dates back to ancient times. It was very popular in the Middle Ages, when the big medieval kitchens of grand houses and castles often had spits in their hearths for cooking large quantities of meat. A servant, typically a boy, sat next to the spit, turning the handle during the course of the day. He was known as the 'spit boy' or 'spit jack'.

Over the years, a whole range of other mechanisms have been employed to turn the spit, including dogs on treadmills, clockwork gearing, water wheels and steam power. There's no reason for you not to get inventive with your own spit-roast, though I find doing it by hand is as good a way as any.

The rate at which the spit needs to turn depends on how hot the fire is and how far away the meat is from it. But the turning should be more or less continuous. Most of the spit-roast meats you'll find for sale at festivals, fairs and fetes are cooked on gas-burning rotisseries. These tend to be made of stainless steel and glass with a bank of gas burners down their length. They usually have an electric motor, which turns the meat slowly. Practical to use and easy to clean, they're an almost foolproof way of cooking a whole carcass.

A wood-fire spit is a different beast altogether. It asks for a little bit more thought and commitment but will give you uniquely delicious results. Such a spit requires hand-cranking and therefore constant person-power to keep it in motion. Although some hand spits have a mechanism by which the spit can be locked in position at various points during the rotation, you do not want to leave a piece of meat in one position for more than a few minutes or it will become too hot on one side and too cool on the other.

Purpose-made wood-fire spits tend to be rudimentary contraptions. In its most basic form, a spit can be nothing more than two hefty bars of metal stuck into the ground, supporting a third horizontal bar between them. The uprights are usually fitted with brackets at different heights to enable the horizontal bar to be raised or lowered with ease. These brackets also allow the horizontal bar to turn. The photograph on the previous page shows the design that we have used at River Cottage with much success. Any metal worker or blacksmith will be able to recreate something similar for you, or you may be able to do it yourself.

Large wood fires are established below the spit – although not directly beneath the meat, in order to avoid scorching. When the fire is hot, the carcass – be it a pig, lamb, goat, deer or chicken – is fixed to the horizontal bar and set above the fire. As long as the fire is fed and the spit turned, the meat will cook. Of course, the bigger the carcass, the longer this will take.

Setting up

The size of the carcass is key. It doesn't want to be too big or it will take too long to cook – or might not fit on the spit at all. A good weight for a pig is anywhere between 35 and 50kg. This will feed 30–50 people with ease. Most lambs have a dead weight of 20–30kg and will feed at least 30 people.

It's really important to fix the carcass to the spit as securely as you can. If it's loose, the spit will turn but the meat won't. The best approach is to push the spit rod, which should feature a series of pre-drilled holes along its length, right through the centre of the carcass. In the case of a whole animal, this means quite literally in through its arse and out through its mouth. You can then push heavy skewers through the carcass horizontally, passing them through the holes in the rod and out the other side. It can be a bit tricky to know exactly where to insert the skewers in order to get them through the holes, but a tape measure can help you estimate where each hole will be once the spit is inside the carcass.

You want a spit rod with at least six of these holes, and heavy skewers at least 60cm long with a spike on one end and a turn on the other. Have some steel wire on hand too, for additional fastenings. I sometimes wire the feet of the carcass to the spit, for example.

If you're roasting a pig, one of your goals is good crackling. To help ensure this, once the pig is mounted on the spit, use a sharp Stanley knife to score the skin. Set the blade at 2mm so that it will penetrate the skin and enter the fat beneath without slicing into the meat. Score in parallel lines, about 2cm apart, all over the skin.

I don't really feel the need to embellish a spit-roast carcass with spices, marinades or rubs. The depth of flavour comes from the meat itself, thanks to the slow cooking

and the complex flavour the wood smoke leaves behind as it passes over the meat. Whatever animal I'm roasting, I simply rub the carcass all over with olive oil before applying plenty of salt and pepper.

Getting the spitted carcass on to the uprights over the fires is most definitely a two-person job, so make sure you ask for help.

Wood for the fires

Spit-roasting a whole animal takes time – often many hours – so ensure you have enough wood to complete the task. How much wood is enough? Well, it's impossible to be precise but a 50kg pig might need 12 hours' cooking. That's a lot of fuel. Even a smaller pig will need 8–10 hours; and cooking time will be at least 6 hours for a goat, lamb or deer carcass, or around 2 hours for a few chickens.

Given that spit-roasting isn't something you do every day, I'd order a big load of dry, well-seasoned logs for the occasion. It won't hurt if you have some left over, but you don't want to run out.

Fires and cooking

The initial temperature of the meat has a massive bearing on cooking time. A carcass straight from the fridge will have a core temperature of 2–3°C – not much above freezing. Heating that up is going to take an awful lot of time and fuel. It makes sense to let the carcass come up to cool room temperature before you begin cooking, as this will speed up the process considerably. With a large carcass, this might mean leaving it out of the fridge overnight. If this isn't possible (in very hot weather, for example), you'll need to factor in that extra time on the fire.

Start your fires at least an hour before you plan to begin cooking, using the basic technique discussed on pp.26–7. As I have said, you should avoid having a fire directly under the carcass. If you do, any fat that drips will flare up, scorching the meat. It's better and more effective to have a fire on either side of the carcass instead, each one extending to the same length as the carcass but not passing directly underneath it. These can be directly on the ground or they can be contained in long, narrow fire baskets, halved oil drums or something similar.

One advantage of having the fires a little offset from the carcass is that you don't have to let the flames die down before you begin cooking. Since you will need to feed the fire while you roast, this would be impractical anyway.

It's best to expose the meat to a high heat initially, with faster rotations, in order to drive some heat into the carcass – this is the equivalent of the brief, hot 'sizzle' you might give a roasting joint of meat in the oven. Once it's cooking nicely, the spit can be raised and the rate at which it's rotated slowed.

You'll need to make sure the heat is hitting its target. A breeze can dramatically effect the cooking time, blowing away the heat rising up from the fire before it reaches the meat above. If there's a breeze, I recommend making a windbreak of some sort, from a non-flammable material. I find metal sheets make the best windbreaks because they also reflect the heat back towards the meat as it's cooking. Thin, mild steel sheets are ideal and sheets of galvanized roofing tin work well too.

You will find that some areas of the carcass require more cooking than others. Deep in the shoulders and the thickest part of the legs will need a lot, for example. You can build up the fires around those areas with a view to driving more heat in, or else let the fires die back below faster-cooking parts (which may be easier).

In the case of lamb or venison, it's worth basting the meat with cider or water during cooking, particularly if it looks dry. The moisture on the surface will help keep the moisture within. A big bunch of woody herbs makes a good basting brush.

If you are cooking a pig, you will, of course, want to make sure that the skin turns to golden crackling – there is no greater gift. If the pig is almost cooked and the crackling has yet to crackle, lower the height of the spit and build up the fire with smaller bits of dry wood. A good burst of intense heat should cause the skin to puff and crackle. Be sure to keep the pig revolving or you may burn the skin.

To ensure the meat is cooked through to the centre, I recommend using a digital probe thermometer. This way you can check that all parts of the carcass have reached the correct temperature. Make sure you get a temperature reading from deep in the shoulder of at least 70°C before you stop cooking.

Carving

When the meat is cooked, it's time to take it off the spit and think about the carving. There's no 'right' way to do this: ultimately you just want to get that lovely, wood-roast meat off the bone and serve it while it's still hot. It can be quicker and easier if two people work together side by side. As long as your fire is still going and you can keep the meat warm as you carve, there's no real need to rush.

Have ready a large, sturdy surface for carving the meat. A strong trestle table covered in a clean oilcloth or several layers of foil works well. You might also want to set a grill over one of the fires, to finish off any meat that wasn't cooked through.

Lift the carcass by its spit and move it to the waiting table. This will require at least two people – and remember that at this point everything's going to be very hot. Allow the meat to rest for 20–30 minutes before carving. This will give you time to bring out salads, bread and other accompaniments.

Some chefs like to wear latex gloves for carving, to protect their hands from immediate heat and keep the grease off – but it's optional. Remove the skewers, the

spit and any other wires or fastenings from the carcass and set these aside. Have a large cutting board on hand and several large deep roasting trays, along with a sharp knife, carving fork, foil, and some hot water and a clean cloth to wipe your work surface and table as you carve.

If you've roasted a pig, cut away the crackling, break it into bits and get it into a roasting tray. Once the tray is full, cover it with foil and keep it warm by the fire.

Start by cutting away one of the shoulders. Place it on your board and slice the meat across the grain. Rotate the shoulder as you carve to get the meat from all sides. It can be fiddly round the shoulder blade, but persevere. If the meat is not as cooked as you'd like around the bone, set it on the grill over the fire for a bit.

Give your board and table a wipe down and move on to the loin on the same side of the carcass. Slice along the length of the backbone and then across the top of the ribs. With a bit of teasing and knife work, you'll be able to remove the whole loin in one piece. Place this on the cutting board, and slice it across the grain into thick rounds. Place the sliced loin in a tray, then cover and keep warm. Wipe down your board and table.

Still working on the same half of the carcass, cut away the back leg and set it down on your board. Cut the meat across the grain into shards and slices. You'll have to do your best to negotiate the bulky bone in the leg – again, if the meat is not quite cooked in some parts, grill it over the fire.

Now remove all the meat from the ribs, and the belly – this is exceptionally tender and incredibly juicy. Under the ribs you'll find the tenderloins or fillets. They're small but delicious, so don't forget about them.

In the case of a pig, the head can be taken off and placed on a platter for your guests to pick at, or you can carve it up, ears and all. There's plenty of meat to be found in the cheeks and down to the snout.

Now repeat the process on the other side of the carcass, filling and covering trays, and keeping them warm by the fire. Around these main primal cuts you'll find all sorts of other delicious morsels on the carcass. Just keep going until you've cleaned the bones.

Leftovers

If you're cooking a whole carcass, you'll almost certainly have some meat left over. Make sure you have some large food bags or fridge containers to hand for this. Get the meat in the fridge as soon as it has cooled. It will keep there for up to 3 days, or you can freeze it for longer. It can be used in sandwiches and salads, simmered into a mean curry or chopped up and fried until crispy then scattered on soups or risottos. (Leftover roast lamb can be used to make a fantastic shepherd's pie.) The bones from the carcass should not be wasted either: simmer at least some of them with some chopped onion, celery and carrot to make a smoky stock.

Planning a 'pig party'

If you decide you want to roast an entire pig (or other whole animal) for friends or family, then planning is essential. This rough time line will help you get organised.

At least 2 weeks ahead

- Fix the date. A warm, dry weekend or bank holiday would be ideal!

- Decide on the spot to site your spit-roast: it should be on flat, even ground, away from trees, sheds, fences or other potentially flammable structures. You'll need plenty of space for the spit and fires, plus room for a table to carve on, and somewhere for plates, bread and other sides.

At least a week ahead

- Fashion or buy a spit and order your wood, making sure you have somewhere to keep it dry until the big day.

- Order your carcass from a good butcher or farming friend, or direct from the abattoir. Free-range or organic meat will taste better. If you're planning on cooking a pig, ask for the back legs to be set forward under the belly for ease of handling. The front trotters can either be bound together under the chin of the pig or wired to the spit at the head end.

The day before

- Take delivery of your carcass. Keep it in a cool place overnight but not in the fridge.

- Set up your spit.

- Plan your cooking times for tomorrow. Allow 8–12 hours for a pig, 6–8 hours for a lamb, 6 hours for a goat or deer carcass, and 2 hours for chickens. If you're planning on serving a big pig at lunchtime, you'll need to organise a shift system for turning the spit through the small hours; if that doesn't sound appealing, plan your feast for the evening instead.

- Prepare accompaniments as far as you possibly can today: buy bread rolls, make apple sauce and coleslaw, mix salad dressings, etc.

On the day

- Get all your tools and equipment in place so that as you cook, and when you come to serve the meat, nothing's too far away.

- Start cooking at your planned time – and enjoy yourself!

Slow-barbecuing

Although I love the simplicity of a campfire on the ground
or the primal thrill of cooking in an earth oven, there are times when I hanker for the flavour and texture of slow-cooked barbecue food.

The word 'barbecue' is often used as another term for campfire or open-fire cooking but I'm talking about something a bit different here: slow-cooking meat in an enclosed, smoky space. This kind of barbecue is traditional to the American Deep South where, for some, it's been a way of life for generations. Barbecue subculture extends from North Carolina right down the coast to Texas and beyond. From state to state, there are variations in meat, marinades and accompaniments but there's one thing that binds them all together: a lengthy, smoky cooking process that results in uniquely savoury deliciousness. We are talking sweet, fall-apart beef brisket, cooked gently for 20 hours or more. Or lightly cured pig's cheeks, smoked slowly until they collapse on the grill; or sticky short ribs where the meat just falls off the bone.

The offset smoker and the kamado

There are two pieces of kit that work well for this type of cooking. The first is the 'horizontal offset smoker' – a contraption probably devised and pioneered by oil-field workers in Texas and Oklahoma. An offset smoker comprises a barrel-shaped, lidded chamber where the food is both smoked and cooked, with a firebox fixed to one side (hence 'offset') and a chimney rising from the other (pictured opposite). A fire is built in the firebox, so that the heat is next to, rather than directly below, the food. Hot air and smoke pass through an opening into the cooking chamber, where they flow around the food, and out through the chimney.

The other piece of kit I've used with great success is a 'kamado'-style ceramic barbecue. The egg-shaped design is based on an ancient type of Japanese cooking stove – kamado is, in fact, the Japanese word for 'stove'. A mushikamado is the name given to a portable or movable kamado, and this is the type that has become especially popular with outdoor-cooking enthusiasts (pictured on pp.226 and 230).

Firing up the barbecue

You can control the heat and smoke flow by adjusting the air intake dampers of your offset barbecue or kamado. Opening the dampers lets more oxygen in, which will produce a hotter fire. It's then possible to close them partially or completely, in order to bring the heat right down, so fish, meat or vegetables can be smoked slowly, over a hardwood of your choice, for several hours.

Make sure there's not an excess of ash in the base of your kamado or in the firebox of your offset smoker, as this can block airflow, thus inhibiting the fire.

Fires for kamados and offset smokers are lit in very much the same way as any regular fire in this book (see pp.26–30). Typically the fire is fed with lumpwood charcoal, which offers a long, slow and consistent burn time – which is what you require for long, slow cooking. Smoke is added by way of wood chips or small bits of hardwood. Chips and wood can be soaked in water first to prolong the period of time they smoke for (i.e. it delays combustion).

Don't hesitate to check on the progress of your barbecue. Lifting the lid is perfectly fine. It's not like opening the oven door on a sponge cake. You'll get a small drop in temperature but it will soon be rectified once the lid is closed again.

Getting used to either bit of kit takes a little practice; in particular, learning how to control the heat is key. But once you've nailed it, you too could become a 'pit master' – a term used to describe someone who has mastered the dark, often smoky, art of Southern-style barbecue.

P.S. For the offset smoker

With an offset smoker, which is less well insulated than a kamado, the end nearest the firebox is always the hottest. So in addition to feeding the fire, you also need to rotate the food periodically to ensure it cooks evenly.

P.P.S. For the kamado

Kamados burn wood (small logs, because of the kamado's size) or charcoal and, thanks to modern ceramics, are incredibly well insulated, which means they are perfect for cooking food gently for extended periods.

The kamado's advanced dampers mean you can adjust the heat with precision. Kamados also usually come with a hefty ceramic 'indirect cooking plate' that can be placed over the fire and beneath (or in place of) the grill. The plate generalises the heat from the fire and allows you to cook food at a constant, even temperature without charring.

But kamado barbecues aren't just for slow, steady cooking. When they're topped up with fuel and the dampers are open, they can produce a quite extraordinary level of heat. Temperatures of 600–700°C are not uncommon. So for searing meat rapidly, blistering vegetables in an instant, or roasting fish fast, they are almost unrivalled. Their cast-iron grills will leave flavoursome charred stripes on steaks and burgers and, because of their hinged lids, it is possible to cook pizzas in them (on the ceramic plate) in the same way that you might in a wood-burning oven.

Smoky pork sausages
with mustard and rosemary glaze

In this recipe, the sausages hot-smoke and roast at the same time and end up tasting incredible. Use the best sausages you can find, and make sure they are nice and fatty so they will soak up the smoky flavours and stay gorgeously succulent.

Serves 4

1 heaped tbsp Dijon mustard
1 tbsp olive oil
1 tbsp soft brown sugar
4–5 sprigs of rosemary, leaves picked

12 free-range or organic pork
 sausages
Sea salt and freshly ground
 black pepper

With the dampers open, start a fire in your smoker or kamado (see pp.228–31). Once the kindling is burning well, build up the fire with charcoal or hardwood. Allow the fuel to burn for 25–30 minutes with the dampers open then, when the flames have died down and you have nice hot embers, add some smoking chips, or a few more lumps of charcoal or hardwood. Shut the lid and partially or completely close the dampers, to reduce the air intake and lower the temperature.

While the smoker/kamado is heating, make the glaze for the sausages: combine the mustard, olive oil and brown sugar in a small bowl and season with salt and pepper. Roughly chop the rosemary leaves and stir into the glaze.

Place the sausages on a tray, spoon the glaze over them and turn to coat. Place in the fridge until you're ready to cook them.

Set the sausages on the grill and close the lid. Cook the sausages for 15–20 minutes, turning once or twice.

Now lift the lid and open the dampers. The temperature will rise and you can caramelise the sausages for a few minutes over this more intense heat.

To check the sausages are done, cut one open to check it is steaming hot and cooked inside. Transfer them to a warm plate and allow to stand for 5 minutes before serving. You can squash the sausages into buns or serve them alongside a big, hearty root vegetable salad.

Barbecued pork shoulder

This is my version of classic pulled pork. I use the top section of the shoulder, sometimes called the whole spare rib, and I keep it on the bone. Before it goes into the barbecue, I always brine the meat for 24 hours. This helps to keep the pork really moist and gives it an incredible depth of flavour. It does, I admit, turn the recipe into a two-day project – but it's well worth it.

Serves 8–10

1 free-range or organic spare rib joint of pork, on the bone

For the brine
2 litres cloudy apple juice
500g salt
1 tbsp cracked black peppercorns
4–5 sprigs of rosemary
12 bay leaves, torn

For the barbecue sauce
2 tbsp English mustard
4 tbsp red wine vinegar
150ml tomato ketchup
1½ tbsp Worcestershire sauce
2 tbsp soft brown sugar
4 garlic cloves, peeled and grated
Sea salt and freshly ground
    black pepper

Combine the ingredients for the brine in a large plastic tub, stirring so that the salt is dissolved. Add the pork and weigh it down with a large plastic food bag filled with brine, so it is completely submerged. Cover and leave in a cool place for 24 hours.

After the allotted time, remove the pork and pat it dry. Discard the brine.

With the dampers open, start a fire in your smoker or kamado (see pp.228–31). Once the kindling is burning well, build up the fire with charcoal or hardwood. If you are using a kamado, make sure you have the indirect cooking plate fitted so it can heat up, and position the grill above the plate.

Allow the fuel to burn for 25–30 minutes with the dampers open then, when the flames have died down and you have nice hot embers, add some smoking chips, or a few more lumps of charcoal or hardwood. Shut the lid and close the dampers partially or completely, to reduce the air intake and lower the temperature. You're looking for a cooking temperature of 110°C.

If I'm using a kamado, I will now set a large foil baking dish, half-filled with water, on the plate under the grill to catch the fat and juices as they drip; this creates moisture in the chamber too. You can do the same thing in an offset smoker, placing the dish below the grill.

Set the pork on the grill and close the lid. Leave the pork to cook for 14–16 hours. You may need to adjust the flow of air, or top up the fuel during cooking in order to keep the temperature consistent. If it drops too low the pork will stop cooking.

When the time is nearly up, make the barbecue sauce: simply combine all the ingredients in a small bowl, adding salt and pepper to taste; set aside.

Use a digital probe thermometer to test the pork's core temperature. It should have reached 85°C and be fork-tender, pulling apart into shreds easily. If not, cook for an hour or two longer. When the meat is fork-tender, take it from the barbecue using tongs and place it on a board or in a large dish. Open up the dampers to increase the heat to 180°C.

Use a knife to remove the pork skin. Then use a brush to paint the meat all over with half the barbecue sauce and return it to the barbecue for 25–30 minutes.

With your tongs, transfer the pork from the barbecue back to the board or dish. Cover it with foil and let it rest for at least 15 minutes.

Using a couple of forks, shred the pork from the bone into shards and strands. (It may be easier to cut the pork into smaller pieces before doing this.) Serve with the remaining barbecue sauce, a sharp, zesty coleslaw and a potato salad.

Cured, smoked pig's cheeks
with salsa verde

Pig's cheeks aren't expensive and a good butcher should be able to get a batch for you – just make sure you ask for whole cheeks, complete with fat and open-grained lighter meat, rather than just the trimmed 'cushion' of darker meat. A light curing is an important step before smoking fish or meat because it draws water out of the flesh, tenderises it and also helps to 'fix' the smoky flavour; it's one reason why these slow-barbecued pig's cheeks are so wonderfully rich and flavourful. Six cheeks might seem like quite a lot but once they are cooked and trimmed, this is just right for six people.

Serves 6

6 free-range or organic pig's
   cheeks

For the dry cure
200g salt
200g demerara sugar
1 tbsp juniper berries, crushed
4 garlic cloves, bashed
4 sprigs of thyme, leaves picked
8 bay leaves, shredded
2 tbsp black peppercorns, cracked

For the salsa verde
1 small garlic clove, peeled
A generous bunch of flat-leaf parsley,
   trimmed of coarse stalks
About 15–20 basil leaves
3–4 sprigs of tarragon, leaves picked
4–5 anchovy fillets in oil
About 1 tsp capers
About 1 tsp Dijon or English mustard
A pinch of sugar
A few drops of lemon juice or
   wine vinegar
2–3 tbsp extra virgin olive oil
Freshly ground black pepper

Combine all the ingredients for the dry cure. Put about one-third of the cure into a large plastic tub and place three of the pig's cheeks on top. Turn them in the cure to ensure they are coated all over. Scatter about another third of the cure over them and add the remaining cheeks. Turn them in the cure to coat, then sprinkle the rest of the cure over the top of everything.

Cover the tub and place in the fridge. Leave the pig's cheeks to cure for 48 hours, turning them once or twice during this time.

Take the pig's cheeks out of the cure. Rinse the cheeks under cold running water, then place them on a clean tea towel and pat dry. (Discard the cure.)

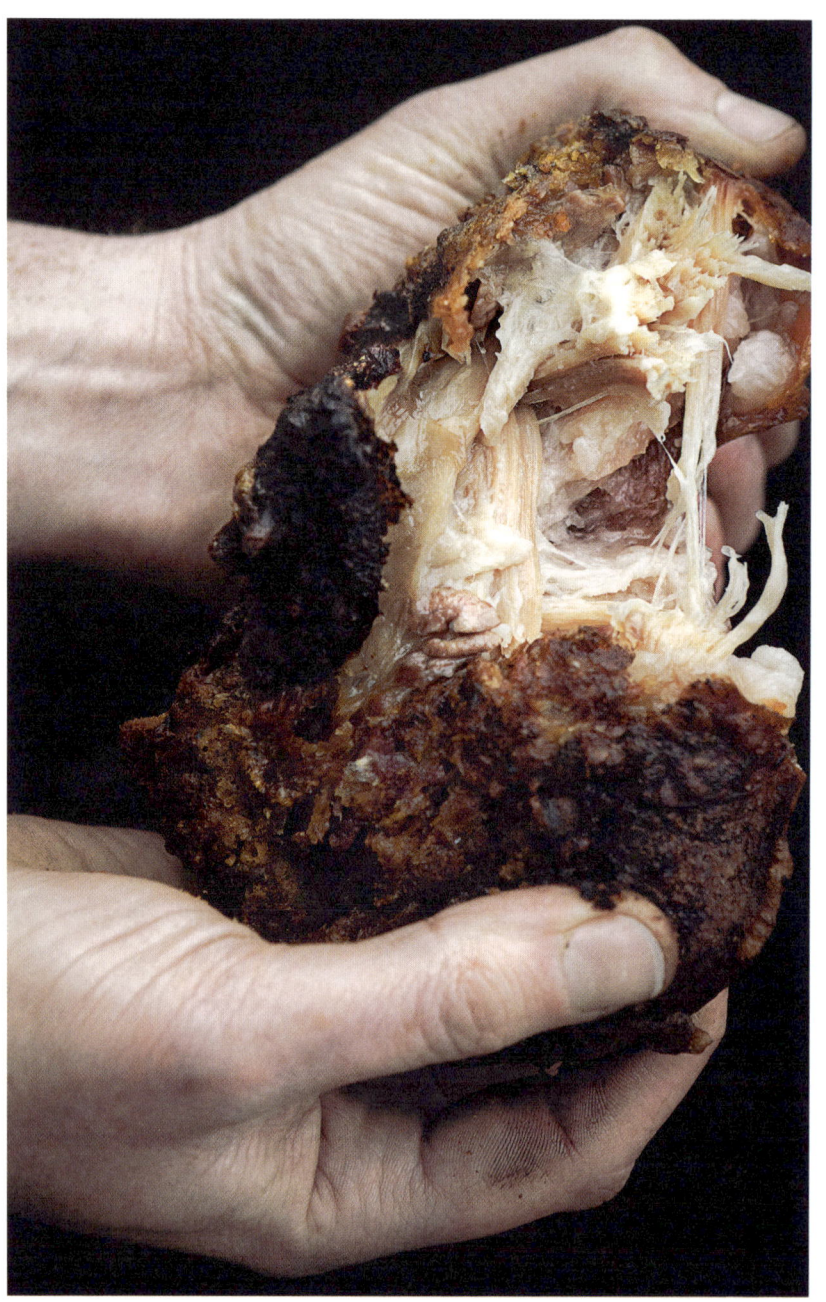

With the dampers open, start a fire in your smoker or kamado (see pp.228–31). Once the kindling is burning well, build up the fire with charcoal or hardwood. If you are using a kamado, make sure you have the indirect cooking plate fitted so it can heat up, and position the grill above the plate.

Allow the fuel to burn for 25–30 minutes with the dampers open then, when the flames have died down and you have nice hot embers, add some smoking chips or a few more lumps of charcoal or hardwood. Shut the lid and close the dampers partially or completely, to reduce the air intake and lower the temperature. You're looking for a cooking temperature of 110°C.

If I am using a kamado, I will now set a large foil baking dish, half-filled with water, on the plate under the grill to catch the fat and juices; this creates moisture in the chamber too. You can do the same thing in an offset smoker, placing the dish below the grill.

Set the pig's cheeks on the grill, skin side down, and close the lid. Leave the cheeks to cook for 12–14 hours or until they are tender enough to break apart easily with a spoon. You may need to adjust the flow of air or top up the charcoal and wood during cooking in order to keep the temperature consistent.

To make the salsa verde, finely chop the garlic on a board. Add the herbs, anchovies and capers and chop the ingredients together until well mixed and fairly fine in texture. Transfer to a bowl and mix in the mustard, sugar, lemon juice or vinegar and some pepper, plus enough olive oil to give a glossy, spoonable consistency, tasting and tweaking the mixture as you go. (This sauce is best made immediately before serving but it will keep for a few days in a sealed jar, in the fridge.)

Use tongs to transfer the pig's cheeks to a warmed platter. Remove the skin and excess fat and discard (or, if you're game, you can eat it too). Slice the pig's cheeks and serve with the salsa verde and some potato and celeriac mash.

Barbecued beef short ribs
with a beer and molasses glaze

Beef short ribs are a lovely slow-barbecue cut. They can take strong flavours – like the rich, complex beer and molasses here – and they cook to delicious tenderness. With their natural bone 'handle', they're perfect to pick up and nibble. Ask your butcher to cut individual ribs for you.

Serves 6–8

5kg beef short ribs
1 tbsp olive oil
25g butter
1 red onion, peeled and sliced
4 garlic cloves, peeled and grated
1 tbsp dried oregano

1 tbsp tomato purée
1 tbsp molasses
500ml dark beer, ale or stout
Sea salt and freshly ground
    black pepper

With the dampers open, start a fire in your smoker or kamado (see pp.228–31). Once the kindling is burning well, build up the fire with charcoal or hardwood. If you are using a kamado, make sure you have the indirect cooking plate fitted so it can heat up, and position the grill above the plate.

Allow the fuel to burn for 25–30 minutes with the dampers open then, when the flames have died down and you have nice, hot embers, add some smoking chips or a few more lumps of charcoal or hardwood.

Shut the lid and close the dampers partially or completely to reduce the air intake and lower the temperature. You're looking for a cooking temperature of 120°C.

If I'm using a kamado, I will now set a large foil baking dish, half-filled with water, on the plate under the grill to catch the fat and juices as they drip; this creates moisture in the chamber too. You can do the same thing in an offset smoker, placing the dish below the grill.

Rub the ribs with the olive oil and season them with salt and pepper. Place the ribs on the grill and close the lid. Cook for 3 hours.

Meanwhile, make the glaze. Place a medium saucepan over a medium heat on the kitchen hob. Add the butter, followed by the onion, garlic, oregano and some salt and pepper. Cook, stirring regularly, for 15 minutes or until the onion is soft and sweet. Stir in the tomato purée, molasses and beer and bring to the boil. Let bubble until reduced by three-quarters then set aside to cool.

After the ribs have had their initial cook, tear off two large sheets of foil and place one on top of the other to form a double layer. Repeat with two more large sheets to make a second double layer. Take half the ribs from the grill and place them on one of the doubled layers of foil. Paint on or spoon over half the glaze. Wrap up the ribs in the foil, trying to keep them in a layer no more than two ribs deep. Repeat with the remaining foil and ribs.

Place the foil packages on the grill and cook for a further 2 hours, until the meat is super tender.

Remove the ribs and leave them to rest in the foil for 30 minutes. Serve with buttered sweetcorn and a tomato salad dressed with red wine vinegar and salt.

Smoked beef brisket
with a treacle and coriander seed rub

Full of rich and fragrant flavours from the rub, this is a fantastic way to transform an under-appreciated cut of meat. Brisket is a tough cut from the forequarter of the animal, consisting of a 'point end' and a broader 'flat end'. I prefer the point end for this recipe because it is nice and fatty. Brisket is incredibly flavoursome but can be dry and disappointing if it's not cooked properly. It's full of connective tissue (collagen) that needs to be turned gently into gelatine through slow cooking. So take your time and don't let the heat creep up too high.

Serves 8–10

5kg piece of point end brisket, on the bone

For the rub
2 tbsp black treacle
2 tbsp boiling water
1 tbsp soft brown sugar
1 tbsp cracked coriander seeds
6 garlic cloves, peeled and grated
2 tsp dried chilli flakes
1 tbsp fine sea salt
1 tbsp black peppercorns, cracked

Combine all the ingredients for the rub in a bowl. Use your hands to massage the rub into the beef, making sure it gets worked in on all sides. Set aside in the fridge until ready to cook.

With the dampers open, start a fire in your smoker or kamado (see pp.228–31). Once the kindling is burning well, build up the fire with charcoal or hardwood. If you are using a kamado, make sure you have the indirect cooking plate fitted so it can heat up, and position the grill above the plate.

Allow the fuel to burn for 25–30 minutes with the dampers open then, when the flames have died down and you have nice hot embers, add some smoking chips or a few more lumps of charcoal or hardwood. Shut the lid and close the dampers partially or completely to reduce the air intake and lower the temperature. You're looking for a cooking temperature of 110°C.

If I'm using a kamado, I will now set a large foil baking dish, half-filled with water, on the plate under the grill to catch the fat and juices as they drip; this creates moisture in the chamber too. You can do the same thing in an offset smoker, placing the dish below the grill.

Set the brisket on the grill and close the lid. Leave the meat to cook for 20–24 hours or until it is very tender. You will need to adjust the flow of air and top up the fuel

during cooking in order to keep the temperature consistent. If you leave a digital probe thermometer in the beef as it cooks you will be able to see its core temperature climb gradually. When it reaches 65–70°C the temperature will plateau and can even fall. This is known as 'the stall' and is caused by the evaporation of moisture from within the meat. Once the moisture has been driven off, the temperature will begin to rise again.

Once the core temperature of the meat has reached 85–88°C, remove it from the barbecue, wrap loosely in foil and allow to rest for an hour or so before carving.

Carve the beef and serve with your choice of pickles, mustard, mashed potato and a few glasses of cold cider.

Smoky aubergine tacos

Like meat, vegetables really benefit from the slow-and-smoky cooking treatment. Aubergines are particularly suited to it, because they respond well to a lengthy cooking time. I like to drop the temperature low for this recipe, to give the aubergines and garlic maximum time in the barbecue, allowing them to soften beautifully while taking on a wonderful smokiness. You can double the quantities if you're planning a feast.

Serves 4–6

4 large aubergines
2 whole garlic bulbs
2 tsp ground cumin
2 tsp ground coriander
1–2 tsp dried chilli flakes
2 tbsp olive oil
Sea salt and freshly ground
    black pepper

To assemble and serve
12 small soft corn or wheat tortillas
1 ripe avocado
Limes, for squeezing
150g mature Cheddar, grated
1 small red onion, peeled and diced
4 tbsp mayonnaise, mixed with 4 tbsp
    harissa (try my version on p.132)

With the dampers open, start a fire in your smoker or kamado (see pp.228–31). Once the kindling is burning well, build up the fire with charcoal or hardwood. If you are using a kamado, make sure you have the indirect cooking plate fitted so it can heat up, and position the grill above the plate.

Let the fuel burn for 25–30 minutes with the dampers open then, when the flames have died down and you have hot embers, add some smoking chips or a few more lumps of hardwood. Shut the lid and adjust the dampers to reduce the air intake and lower the temperature. You're looking for a cooking temperature of 120°C.

Place the aubergines and garlic bulbs on the rack, close the lid and cook for 1 hour.

Lift the lid and remove the aubergines and garlic to a platter (carefully as they'll be hot and fragile). Leave to cool for 10 minutes, then slice them all in half. Scoop, squeeze and generally encourage their contents out into a large bowl. Add the cumin, coriander, chilli flakes, olive oil and plenty of salt and pepper. Mix well. Taste the mix and make sure you're happy with the balance of flavours.

Warm the tortillas on the grill of the barbecue. Halve, stone and peel the avocado, then slice. To serve, divide the smashed, smoked aubergine mixture between the tortillas, then top each with a few slices of avocado, a squeeze of lime, a sprinkle of grated Cheddar, a scattering of red onion and a spoonful of harissa mayo.

Useful Things

Directory

One of the lovely things about cooking outside is using your initiative, up-cycling and making do and mend. Keeping things natural and simple and trusting your instincts nearly always pays off, but sometimes you'll need a little help and just a bit of kit.

For firewood and charcoal:
thelondonlogcompany.blogspot.com
oxfordcharcoal.co.uk
benshortcharcoal.co.uk/
treewoodharvesting.com

For barbecues, kamados and fire bowls:
kadai.co.uk
biggreenegg.co.uk
ofyr.co.uk

For wood ovens and wood oven kits:
thestonebakeovencompany.co.uk

For cast- and spun-iron pots and pans:
cranecookware.com
netherton-foundry.co.uk
dutchovens.co.uk

For axes and knives:
alexpoleironwork.com
poleandhunt.co.uk
prendergastknives.com
blenheimforge.co.uk
opinel.com/en
ryderandhope.com

For natural clay:
ctmpotterssupplies.co.uk

For fire bricks, cement etc:
shop.vitcas.com

Further reading

Food from the Fire: The Scandinavian Flavours of Open-Fire Cooking
Niklas Ekstedt

Norwegian Wood: Chopping, Stacking and Drying the Scandinavian Way
Lars Mytting

Hunter Gather Cook: Adventures in Wild Food Nick Weston

Fire Food: The Ultimate BBQ Cookbook Christian Stevenson

Finding Fire: Cooking at its Most Elemental Lennox Hastie

The Ultimate Wood Fired Oven Cookbook Genevieve Taylor

Gather: Everyday Seasonal Food from a Year in our Landscapes
Gill Meller

Time: A Year and a Day in the Kitchen
Gill Meller

McGee on Food and Cooking: An Encyclopedia of Kitchen Science, History and Culture Harold McGee

Acknowledgements

I'd really like to thank Hugh Fearnley-Whittingstall for the encouragement, knowledge, support, generosity and friendship he's shown to me over the years we've been working together. It's been such an adventure, and long may it continue.

Thanks must go to everyone at River Cottage, including, but not limited to, Stewart Dodd, Gelf Alderson, Andrew Tyrrell, Conner Reed, Mark McCabe, Will Livingstone, Jess Upton, Lucy Brazier, Lucy Lomas, Steve Lamb and everyone else who works so hard to make it such an inspiring place.

Thanks to the ever fabulous Nikki Duffy for all the help and guidance with this book; I'm not quite sure if I could have done it without you.

Thank you to Gavin Kingcome for the stunning pictures. This has been such a great project to work on, and it's even better to see it all captured so beautifully for the pages of this book.

Special thanks to Xa Shaw Stewart at Bloomsbury; it's a pleasure to work with such a calm, collected, confident editor. I'm also very grateful to Natalie Bellos, Ellen Williams, Jen Hampson and Gary Hayes, who have all helped to make this book such a joy.

Thanks to Janet Illsley and to Will Webb for your uncompromising attention to detail. I've thoroughly enjoyed working with you both again.

As always, my thanks must go to my agent, Antony Topping, and his team at Greene and Heaton.

Thanks, also, to Romy Fraser and everyone at Trill Farm; and to Neil White, Christian Stevenson, Sam Lomas, Kayla Nelson and the teams at Coombe Farm and Pipers Farm.

Lastly, the biggest thank you goes to my wife, Alice, and my daughters, Isla and Coco. Thank you for the fires we've made together and for the fires we'll make in the future.

Index

Page numbers in *italic* refer to the illustrations

River Cottage Handbooks

Seasonal, Local, Organic, Wild

FOR FURTHER INFORMATION AND
TO ORDER ONLINE, VISIT
RIVERCOTTAGE.NET